Florida's Indians from Ancient Times to the Present

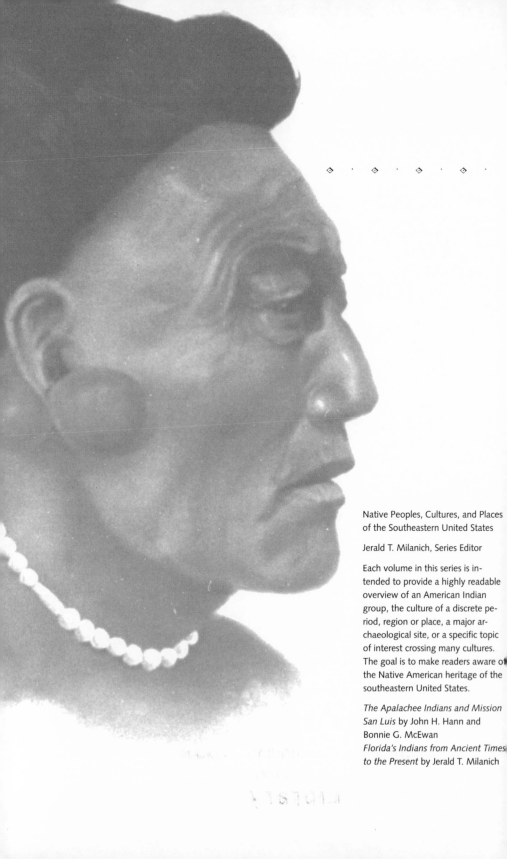

◇ · ◇ · ◇ · ◇ ·

Native Peoples, Cultures, and Places
of the Southeastern United States

Jerald T. Milanich, Series Editor

Each volume in this series is intended to provide a highly readable
overview of an American Indian
group, the culture of a discrete period, region or place, a major archaeological site, or a specific topic
of interest crossing many cultures.
The goal is to make readers aware of
the Native American heritage of the
southeastern United States.

*The Apalachee Indians and Mission
San Luis* by John H. Hann and
Bonnie G. McEwan
*Florida's Indians from Ancient Times
to the Present* by Jerald T. Milanich

Jerald T. Milanich

# Florida's Indians from Ancient Times to the Present

University Press of Florida
Gainesville
Tallahassee
Tampa
Boca Raton
Pensacola
Orlando
Miami
Jacksonville

This publication has been financed in part with historic preservation grant assistance provided by the Bureau of Historic Preservation, Division of Historical Resources, Florida Department of State, assisted by the Historic Preservation Advisory Council. However, the contents and opinions do not necessarily reflect the views and opinions of the Florida Department of State, nor does the mention of trade names or commercial products constitute endorsement or recommendation by the Florida Department of State.

 A Florida Heritage Publication

03  02  01  00  99  98  C  6  5  4  3  2  1

03  02  01  00  99  98  P  6  5  4  3  2  1

LIBRARY OF CONGRESS CATALOGING-IN-PUBLICATION DATA

Florida's Indians from ancient times to the present / Jerald T. Milanich
p. cm. —(Native peoples, cultures, and places of the southeastern United States)
Includes bibliographical references.
ISBN 0-8130-1598-7 (cl.: alk. paper). — ISBN 0-8130-1599-5 (pbk.: alk. paper)
1. Indians of North America—Florida. 2. Florida—Antiquities.
I. Title. II. Series.
E78.F6M555  1998  97-45841
975.9'01—dc21

The University Press of Florida is the scholarly publishing agency for the State University System of Florida, comprising Florida A&M University, Florida Atlantic University, Florida International University, Florida State University, University of Central Florida, University of Florida, University of North Florida, University of South Florida, and University of West Florida.

University Press of Florida
15 Northwest 15th Street
Gainesville, FL 32611
http://nersp.nerdc.ufl.edu/~upf

# Contents

Apalachee Indians in Louisiana, photographed ca. 1914

## Past and Present

The September 1996 issue of the *Florida Anthropologist* contained a re-markable snapshot in its "Featured Photograph" section (p. 163). Taken about 1914 in Bayou Cypre, Louisiana, the black-and-white image shows five great-great-grandchildren of John Baptiste Vallery, "identified as an Apalache[e] Indian in Catholic baptismal records in Natchitoches, Louisiana."

Why is this eighty-five-year-old photograph of Apalachee Indians so extraordinary? Why would an early twentieth-century record of five American Indians be of interest today? The answers to those questions are in large part what this book is about.

The first Indians came into the region that is now Florida 12,000 years ago. The land they found and from which they wrested their livelihood was a land far different from the Florida of today. It was the end of the Pleistocene, the Great Ice Age, and Florida was cooler and drier. Having huge amounts of water tied up in glaciers around the world meant that sea level was as much as 300 feet lower than it is today. As a consequence, Florida's total land area was about twice what it is presently.

As human populations increased and as the climate of Florida became more like it is at present, the native societies also changed. By about 3000 B.C., the warmer and wetter conditions had resulted in the appearance of modern vegetation communities. Sea level also had risen nearly to its modern level. The number of people continued to increase, and by the time the first Europeans invaded the land Juan Ponce de León had named *La Florida*, literally hundreds of different Indian societies lived in every part of the state.

One of those groups was the Apalachee Indians, whose home was in the eastern panhandle. Some of the most important Apalachee Indian towns, including their precolumbian capitals, were in Leon County. Indeed one of the most important archaeological sites in Florida—Lake Jackson, a precolumbian Apalachee Indian capital—is quite near Tallahassee, Florida's present-day state capital. Many other native groups lived elsewhere in the state, from the western panhandle to the northeast coast and southward to the Keys.

But the lives these native peoples had carved out of their natural settings would soon be threatened and ultimately destroyed. Florida and the rest of the Americas drew colonists from Europe, especially from Spain, France, and later Great Britain. Conquistadors, entrepreneurs, soldiers, missionary friars, and settlers all came to Florida seeking wealth, souls to save, and new lands to colonize.

Two centuries after the founding of the first European town, St. Augustine, the European colonization of Florida had resulted in the destruction of the native populace. By 1763 warfare, slave raiding, and especially epidemics of disease had annihilated what had been a population of some 350,000 people at the time Ponce de León first came to Florida in 1513.

European conflicts, which spilled over to rivalries in the Americas, including the southeastern United States, also helped to contribute to the demise of the Florida Indians. When Spain withdrew from St. Augustine and Florida in 1763–64 as a result of a treaty with Great Britain, fewer than 100 Indians remained to accompany the departing Spaniards. And most of those native people were not descendants of the indigenous people who had been there when St. Augustine was founded in 1565. Rather, they were the relatives of South Carolinian, Georgian, and other native groups who had moved southward into Florida during the late colonial period.

During the early eighteenth century, a time when raids on Spanish missions by English-speaking Carolinian militia destroyed most of the existing Indian settlements in northern Florida, some of the Indians fled westward, out of the state. Nearly all disappeared, probably merging with other native societies and losing their own ethnic identities. One remnant population known to have survived into the nineteenth century was a small number of Apalachee Indians, who in 1836 were living on the Red River in Louisiana. Researchers—James Covington in the 1960s and more recently Donald Hunter—have documented the presence of those Red River Apalachee, perhaps the last of the Florida Indians. The few native people taken to Cuba from St. Augustine in 1763–64 did not survive long in their new setting. Only the Apalachee endured, and they apparently ceased to exist sometime in the nineteenth century. Or did they?

The photograph in the *Florida Anthropologist* is proof to the contrary. Those of us who had lamented the final demise of the Florida Indians were wrong. All the indigenous Indians of Florida were not lost under the stifling blanket of colonialism. Recently, descendants of the Apalachee Indians literally walked out of history into the present. Thanks to the research of Donald Hunter and to the Apalachee themselves, the story of these modern Louisiana residents is now being told.

This book is about the Apalachee Indians and their neighbors, people like the Calusa, Tequesta, Jororo, Potano, and Ais, who once made their homes in Florida. It also is about their ancestors and their ancestors' ancestors, a chain of people going back 12,000 years to the first Floridians.

Today in Florida there are other Indians, who also have a proud past and whose stories deserve to be told. These people include the descendants of Creek Indians who began moving into Florida after 1750 and became the Seminole and Miccosukee people. Many modern residents of Florida do not know that the Seminole and the Miccosukee Indians are not descendants of the precolumbian Florida Indians. Their histories, like the histories of all other Floridians living in the state today, lie outside the boundaries of what is rapidly becoming the third largest of the 50 united states.

The 13,000,000 late twentieth-century residents of Florida include not only Seminole and Miccosukee peoples but other Native Americans as well. Like nearly all other Floridians, these Native Americans moved to Florida or were born there in the last century. These modern Florida Indians also are a part of the story told here.

In organizing this book I have chosen to begin at the beginning, the time of the Paleoindians, when perhaps only a few dozen people initially moved into the state in search of food, water, and the other items they needed to sustain their way of life. Soon these earliest Indians were joined by others, and over the next several thousand years, the time of the Archaic cultures, many generations utilized Florida's natural bounty. As the environment changed, so did the native cultures. The first two chapters draw on archaeological and paleoenvironmental evidence to relate what we know about these early people, who would eventually establish settlements throughout Florida.

The next five chapters draw on archaeological investigations to describe the various cultures that developed out of the earlier Archaic cultures by 500 B.C. As we shall see, we can separate these later people into a number of distinctive cultures, each associated with a geographical region. Despite their diversity, which arose in large part because of the different environmental zones in which they lived, these native groups shared many aspects of their lifeways. At least some cultures can be traced forward into the colonial period, a time when European observers recorded information about the native Floridians. Where appropriate, I have drawn on those historical accounts to help interpret and enhance the archaeological record of these post–500 B.C. precolumbian cultures.

The events of the colonial period and the impact of the European presence on the native societies are the focus of the eighth and ninth chapters. For the sixteenth, seventeenth, and early eighteenth centuries, archaeology and history combine to tell us who the people were, how they lived, and what happened to them. The final chapter brings us to the present.

My goal in writing this book is to provide a not-too-long overview, one that will be useful to readers interested in past and present Native Americans and in the history of the Sunshine State. I have tried to keep jargon to a minimum. However, archaeologists do use a lot of names. In order to know who it is we are speaking about, we must be able to refer to the various cultures and the people associated with those cultures. Unfortunately, we have no idea how precolumbian peoples may have referred to themselves. So we assign names, usually but not always names taken from modern places where archaeological investigations into the cultures were first carried out.

As a consequence, we have precolumbian cultures with names like Safety Harbor or Alachua or Caloosahatchee. Nearly all of these names have been in use in archaeological literature for many decades. For the oldest native cultures, those of the Paleoindians and Archaic peoples, we have been even less creative. Their names simply mean "ancient" or "old" Indians.

As much as possible, I promise not to dwell on these archaeological names for the early Florida Indians. For readers who may want to delve more deeply into the intricacies of archaeological and historical interpretations, I have provided a list of additional readings (and I have listed addresses for two web sites that will provide access to a wealth of on-line information for those using the Internet).

On the other hand, I do use a lot of modern place-names. I want to connect the past to the present, to convey that in the very places where we walk, talk, and toil today, Native Americans once did the very same things. It is important to respect that past, just as it is important for us to respect the human diversity that surrounds all of us today. Learning about the past increases our ability to appreciate the present and to plan our future.

## Acknowledgments

Thanks are due Nancy White, Marvin Smith, and the other individuals who reviewed drafts of my manuscript and to the team at the University Press of Florida, especially Ken Scott, who gave me the impetus, and Meredith Morris-Babb, who gave intercontinental encouragement. My colleague Bill Keegan made it possible to complete this project a long way from home. I am grateful to you all.

The Bureau of Historic Preservation, Division of Historical Resources, Florida Department of State, provided a publication subsidy.

# 1    Ancient Floridians

Since at least the 1920s, residents of Florida have been finding Indian artifacts in the bottoms of rivers in the northern part of the state. The Simpson family of High Springs were pioneers in river collecting, diving the depths and wading the shallow portions of the Ichetucknee River long before it became a state park.

One artifact found by the Simpsons would offer dramatic proof of the antiquity of humans in Florida. That artifact—a broken portion of a harpoonlike spear point—was made from the ivory tusk of a mammoth, an elephant which lived in Florida during the Ice Age but became extinct shortly after. Not only was the point made from a mammoth's tusk, it was identical to an ivory artifact found at the Blackwater Draw archaeological site near Clovis, New Mexico. In the 1930s at that site, Paleoindian artifacts were found for the first time in America in association with the bones of extinct Pleistocene animals. Blackwater Draw proved that humans—Paleoindians—lived in the Americas at the end of the Ice Age. The Ichetucknee River point, as well as other artifacts and animal bones found by the Simpsons, showed that Paleoindians were living in Florida at the same time, and they too must have hunted now extinct animals. Today we know that the earliest Paleoindian sites in Florida were occupied 12,000 years ago.

## Collecting the Ichetucknee

As an undergraduate student assistant in the Florida State Museum, then located in the Seagle Building in downtown Gainesville, I had the duty of writing catalogue numbers on the many objects of the Simpson Collection. It was definitely menial labor, but I became interested in the collection, which had been assembled by the Simpson family of High Springs, Florida, and later donated to the museum.

Thirty years later I am back at the museum, which has a new name and is in a new building. I often have occasion to refer to artifacts in the Simpson Collection, using the very numbers I wrote three decades ago. Of great importance are the many bone tools from the Ichetucknee River.

Recently, I ran across a charming article written by Mrs. H. H. Simpson, Sr., and published in 1935:

Until the summer of 1927 our collection consisted of flint and stone implements, shell ornaments and pottery, but in June of that year began the addition of a section that to us is more interesting, if possible, than any of the others. At that time we found, by accident, a clear river [the Ichetucknee] about sixteen miles from our home. I would have to be an artist to describe the beauty of the place. At all times the river is perfectly transparent. In the sandy portions of the bed of the river vari-colored grasses grow, waving back and forth, the different colors blending and forming a beautiful under-water moving picture in the swift current. . . . The day we found it we waded in the clear water close to the bank, and could see, out in the deeper water, pockets in the rocky bottom which were full of bones of different shapes and sizes. Swimming out and diving Clarence brought up handfuls of the material for examination. Some of the smaller pieces were smooth, and shaped as though made by hand but they were such small fragments that we couldn't arrive at a definite conclusion. We returned on a second trip hoping to find some large pieces of what we suspected were bone implements of a vanished race of people. As we stood on the bank and watched him, Clarence dived again and again. In shallow water he picked the bones up with his toes, which have been trained to serve him for various purposes beside the ordinary use of toes. Finally we saw him make a high leap, and run toward shore as fast as he could. Racing to where we stood, and taking a small black object out of his mouth, he exclaimed, excitedly: "Now, I know these things are hand-made!" Upon examining it we found it to be a upper section of a bone artifact, ornamented with lines at the top. . . . We were overjoyed. (*Hobbies* 40[4] (1935):93–94)

## Paleoindians

Who were these Paleoindians, these "ancient Indians," and how did they live? What was the significance of their stone, bone, and ivory artifacts being found with animal bones in the bottom of rivers, not only the Ichetucknee but the other limestone-bottomed rivers of northern Florida like the Santa Fe, Aucilla, and Wacissa?

The Florida Paleoindians were descendants of people who crossed into North America from eastern Asia during the Pleistocene epoch. At that time the oceans of the world were several hundred feet lower than they are today, and Asia and Alaska were connected by a bridge of dry land more than a thousand miles in width. The higher sea levels that followed the Ice Age have covered that bridge, leaving the two continents separated by the narrow Bering Strait.

Exactly when humans crossed Beringia, as the land bridge is known, is still a matter of discussion. What is certain is that it first occurred more than 12,000 years ago. These ancient people rapidly spread throughout the Americas. In North America, including Florida, they lived by roaming over large tracts of land hunting small and large animals and by gathering plants. Among the many species of animals they hunted, some of which are now extinct, were mammoths. We call these nomadic hunters Paleoindians.

The Florida of the Paleoindians would not be recognizable to you or I. Lowered sea levels meant that the coasts were much farther out than they are today, especially along the Gulf of Mexico. As a result, Florida's land area was about twice what it is today; modern Pinellas Peninsula where St. Petersburg is situated was some 50 miles from the Paleoindian shoreline.

Lower sea levels and massive glaciers created a climate that was much drier, and groundwater levels in the interior of the state were greatly below what they are today. Florida was cool and arid; the springs, lakes, rivers, and other wetlands so important at present did not exist. There were some fluctuations in climate, with slightly wetter conditions replacing drier ones, but the area always was much more arid than it is in modern times.

More arid conditions meant that a different array of animals and plants were present. Some of those animals, like mammoths, Pleistocene horses, and a now extinct species of bison, had prospered during the Ice Age but would disappear as the climate warmed and they fell prey to human hunters. Typical vegetation included plants that could live in the dry conditions; scrub oaks, pine forests, open grassy prairies, and savannahs were most common. In the restricted localities where water was present, plants

Florida's shoreline at the time of the Paleoindians and locations of sites

better suited to wetter conditions were found. Because the climate did fluctuate, the vegetative communities in any one location likewise fluctuated over time.

The Paleoindians first lived in Florida during one of the more arid periods. How did the climate affect their way of life? The answer to that question in large part explains why their artifacts are found in the river bottoms of the northern half of Florida.

Like ourselves, the Paleoindians needed water to drink and for other necessities. Because water was in short supply, the places where it was available drew the Paleoindians. These same watering holes attracted animals as well. Such water sources were found in the limestone catchment basins of northern Florida. Although limestone formations are found throughout Florida, it is in the northern half of the state that limestone is common on or near the land surface. Water from rain or ground seepage collected in pockets in the limestone, forming water holes not unlike the watering holes found today in parts of Africa.

At the time of the Paleoindians, what are now the Ichetucknee, Santa Fe, and other northern Florida rivers were not flowing rivers but series of small limestone catchment basins or watering holes. Occasionally, perhaps during slightly less arid periods, surface water collected where clay or marl deposits provided somewhat impermeable catchments. Water also could be found in a few deep sinkholes fed during wetter intervals by springs.

But over time the most consistent watering holes were those in the northern half of the state where the limestone formations reached the surface of the ground and formed catchments. That region is from Tampa Bay north through the western half of peninsular Florida into the panhandle to the Chipola River. Such formations also extend out into what is today the floor of the Gulf of Mexico but was then dry land. It was this limestone region of Florida that drew the Paleoindians.

As noted, the same oases that provided humans with water were used by animals. Consequently, besides being places where people camped, watering holes were sites where animals were ambushed, butchered, and eaten, their remains being discarded along with other debris left by the Paleoindians. Today these camps are in river bottoms and sinkholes. Over two and a half millennia, there must have been thousands of such camps and kill sites. It is no wonder that Paleoindian-age tools and butchered animal bones are found in those rivers and sinkholes.

Now we know who the Paleoindians were and why we find their artifacts and debris in inundated archaeological sites in Florida. What else have we learned about them? Although artifacts picked up from rivers and sinkholes have been important for understanding where Paleoindians once lived and what their environment was like, other types of information must come from the excavation of sites. But if most Paleoindian camps today are underwater, how can they be excavated? The answer is to go in after them. This is exactly what researchers in Florida are doing, combining SCUBA diving and archaeology.

At present the largest of these underwater Paleoindian projects, the Aucilla River Prehistory Project, is taking place in the river of the same name, one of northern Florida's many limestone-bottomed rivers. Under the auspices of the Florida Museum of Natural History and directed by S. David Webb, ARPP has located nearly 40 inundated Paleoindian sites in a short stretch of the river.

## Indiana Jones She Isn't; Archaeologist She Is

For every university-trained archaeologist engaged in research in Florida, there are hundreds of people who make significant contributions to our knowledge of Florida's precolumbian Indians. Often these people contribute their time, money, and expertise to work on projects conceived and led by those of us who work in museums and universities. The reality is that archaeology in North America depends on the contributions of volunteers, avocational archaeologists like Mary Gouchnour Hudson.

What makes an avocational archaeologist? By day Mary, a native of Florida, is a radiation therapist and CPR instructor in Gainesville and a student majoring in anthropology at Santa Fe Community College. But during weekends, vacations, and evenings she does all those things archaeologists do: reads professional journals, participates in field investigations, co-manages the field office, works to raise funding for research, and undertakes public education initiatives.

Most recently she has written articles for the *Aucilla River Times,* the Florida Museum of Natural History's Aucilla River Prehistory Project (ARPP) newsletter, on "Understanding Radiocarbon Dating" and "Water Moccasins and the ARPP." The latter recounts close encounters experienced by ARPP personnel and what to do if bitten. About her participation in the project, Mary writes:

> Why do I return season after season, spending my vacations freezing in October or fighting off swarms of bugs in May? Many of my friends say this is a sickness—digging through dirt and river sludge looking for some old bones and artifacts, living in "primitive" camping conditions out in the middle of nowhere, keeping company with a bunch of scuba divers and science cowboys. Hopelessly afflicted with the same sickness, we all . . . rise before the dawn, shiver and shudder as we step into those cold wet suits, and work hard until dusk, exhausted and starving. At the Aucilla, like the Eagles' "Hotel California," "You can check out any time you like, but you can never leave." . . . As we toil together in search of man and mastodon . . . we share more than a common interest in an exciting scientific expedition. We share enthusiasm, dedication, and the intensity for a great quest. . . . The interaction of various professional scientists, avocational volunteers, students, and financial and political supporters all have their place of importance in the success of this project. . . . Newcomers as well as veterans are actively involved in teaching and learning. . . . This initiates motivation and interaction and . . . promotes much enthusiasm and gratification. (*Aucilla River Times* 9 [1996], p. 15)

A close encounter, Paleoindian style. This skull of an extinct species of bison has a broken stone point sticking into it. When the animal was alive, the tips of its horns were about 3 feet across; the tips of the horn cores, shown here, are only 25 inches apart.

Webb and his research team were originally drawn to the site by reports of Paleoindian tools and animals bones being found there. A short distance away in the Wacissa River, which flows into the Aucilla, sport divers had found the skull of a *Bison antiquus* (a now extinct species of large bison) with a broken stone point in it, dramatic evidence for Paleoindians and Pleistocene animals having lived there at the same time.

Another underwater site excavated by archaeologists is Little Salt Spring in Sarasota County. When Paleoindians camped there, perhaps during a period of less aridity, water collected in the bottom of the sinkhole. Although it was probably too deep for most animals, Paleoindians could lower themselves down into the sink off a ledge to reach the water. This could not have been an easy task, and it points out the importance—and rarity—of water.

Sites like those in the Aucilla River and Little Salt Spring provide evidence of the activities of Paleoindians—we might think of them as small time capsules of information. In addition these sites have yielded artifacts and other evidence that are not found in land sites, such things as wood and bone artifacts, and even plant remains, which would quickly have rotted away if not in water. Excavations in the Aucilla River have produced seeds and rind fragments from wild gourds, evidence that Paleoindians were collecting a plant not previously known even to have been in Florida at such an early time. Preserved hickory nuts have been found, as have carved wooden stakes, perhaps items associated with small, temporary tentlike structures or lean-tos.

The Aucilla River underwater excavations are also providing new information on the animals hunted by the Paleoindians. Analysis of growth rings of mammoth tusks suggests that these animals may have been moving seasonally from north to south and back again. That raises an interesting possibility: did the Paleoindians move with the herds, following them as they made their seasonal treks northward in summer and southward in winter?

An offshoot of excavations by Webb's team is information about the diet of these giant creatures. Hundreds of samples of mammoth digesta, the remains of the plants eaten and then defecated by animals standing in the watering holes, have been preserved. Plant fibers in the digesta not only give clues to the elephants' diet but are indicators of the climate as well. Scientists have even extracted mammoth hormones from the digesta!

Someday, comparisons of digesta samples and skeletons may shed light on the extinction of the elephants. Both pre-Paleoindian samples and samples from Paleoindian occupation are known. Evidence of stress caused by overhunting may show up in the latter, perhaps in dietary changes, through comparison of bone densities, or in the ages of the animals hunted. For instance, as herds became smaller and animals harder to find, the Paleoindians may have become less selective in the animals they hunted, seeking to kill not only easy prey—youngsters or weaker individuals—but healthy adults as well. Only a few short years ago, studies such as these would have been unthinkable.

Careful excavations by divers using techniques modified from land site investigations have recovered a cross section of the animals utilized by the Paleoindians. The list is remarkable and includes both modern species and species that became extinct at the end of the Pleistocene, perhaps in large part because of overhunting by Paleoindians. The extinct animals include the mammoth, bison, giant land tortoise, sloth, tapir, horse, camelids, and a type of box turtle.

That human hunting may have been a major factor in the extinction of many of these animals is suggested by the case of the Pleistocene horse. Essentially the same animal as the horses that thrive in the southeastern United States today, including in wild populations on coastal islands, the Pleistocene horse became extinct during Paleoindian times. Later, in the sixteenth century, horses were reintroduced into the Americas by Europeans. If horses can live here today, why did the Pleistocene horse suffer extinction? Human predation seems a likely cause.

The Florida Paleoindians probably caught or hunted every animal they could. Species identified from Paleoindian sites and still living in Florida today are deer, fish, various turtles, freshwater shellfish, the gopher tortoise, diamondback rattlesnake, raccoon, opossum, rabbit, muskrat, wood ibis, panther, and frogs. Like other people who lived by hunting, gathering, and foraging, the Paleoindians made use of almost everything in their environment. Beyond providing food, these animals also supplied them with furs, ligaments, antlers, bones, teeth, and claws, all raw materials useful to the Paleoindians.

Most likely, when all the evidence is in, we will have learned that these early native peoples hunted and gathered almost everything that was edible or usable, including a variety of plants. And it would not be surprising to learn that Paleoindians living along the coasts used marine foods as well, though such research would have to be carried out at sites on the floor of the Gulf of Mexico, well off the present coast.

What tools did these people use to hunt and butcher animals and process their parts? What did they use to fashion clothing and shelter? Not surprisingly, the lithic and bone tool kits of the Paleoindians do not contain large objects like those of later people, nor is there a huge variety. But that is what we might expect from people who moved frequently from watering hole to watering hole. More surprising is that the tools of the Florida Paleoindians closely resemble those of other Paleoindians as far away as the southwestern United States. The Paleoindian way of life must have developed and spread rapidly across the Americas, with similar tools being used over a continent.

The most easily recognizable Paleoindian artifacts in Florida are lanceolate spear points, most often chipped from chert, a flintlike stone common in limestone formations. Archaeologists have separated these distinctive points into various types based on shape and other characteristics

Paleoindian points. The upper left specimen, 2 ½ inches long, has the classic fluting of a Clovis point.

and have given them names. Most common are Suwannee points, which, like most other Paleoindian points, have their lower portions ground so that the sharp edges do not cut into bindings used to haft the points onto shafts. Hundreds of Suwannee points have been found in Florida, and 92 percent of all those recovered are from the limestone region in the northern half of the state.

Other Paleoindian points also are lanceolate in shape. They include Clovis points—common at Paleoindian sites across the United States outside of Florida—each of which has a distinctive flute running longitudinally up both sides. It is thought that the Clovis points, which make up about 10 percent of all the Paleoindian points found in Florida, and perhaps others of the larger lanceolate points, were hafted by attaching them to a mammoth ivory foreshaft, which in turn was attached to a wooden spear. It was one of these ivory foreshafts that the Simpson family found in the Ichetucknee River and identified as a point.

Some spears were used in conjunction with throwing sticks. Bone-throwing stick weights and bone and shell "triggers"—the latter fitting over the end of the stick to butt against the end of the spear shaft—have come from underwater sites. The use of throwing sticks allowed hunters to cast spears farther and with more force.

For hunting, Paleoindians probably used bolas as well as spears. Several egg-sized, ground stone bola weights were attached to one another with long leather thongs, then thrown at prey. The weighted thongs wrapped around legs or other body parts and helped to bring the animal down.

Although the stone points and ivory foreshafts are the most distinctive and most easily identifiable of the Paleoindian artifacts, other tools are known from a variety of sites. Many of the stone tools are simply made and probably served more than one purpose. It may have been easier to carry a few tools to do many jobs than to carry a larger number of specialized items. Scrapers, small adzes, spokeshaves used to shape shafts, and knives, some of which were hafted, are most common. Other tools include bone pins, bone needles, a fossil shark tooth that had been hafted and used as a knife, socketed antler points, and a socketed bone handle.

A portion of what appears to be a log mortar carved from oak was preserved underwater in the Little Salt Spring site; it probably was used to grind seeds or nuts. An extraordinary artifact from that same site is the head of a nonreturnable, wooden boomerang or throwing stick, also made of oak. Recently several were recovered by University of Miami archaeologists.

Paleoindians were no novices; the tools and accoutrements they made and used were well suited to their way of life. With tools and weapons in hand, small groups of Paleoindians traveled relatively large tracts of land, moving from one watering hole to the next, traveling over what was certainly well-known territory. But their way of life would not last. Changes were afoot, changes that would lead to the development of the Archaic culture after about 7500 B.C.

### The Early Archaic Culture

Changes in Florida's climate began to appear at about 8000 B.C., late in the Paleoindian period. As the Pleistocene ended and the climate became less cool, glaciers began to melt, leading to more rainfall and less arid conditions. Sea level began to rise. In Florida, water sources were no longer in such short supply. People had more places to camp and they could stay longer at each camp.

It was at this same time that some of the animals previously so important to Paleoindian hunters—mammoth, horse, bison, and others—dwindled in number and became extinct. Other sources of food, including smaller game, increased in significance. The old ways of nomadic hunter-gatherers gave way to new patterns of securing food to eat.

These changes are reflected in the archaeological record of the Late Paleoindian culture. The large, lanceolate Paleoindian points no longer were needed and ceased to be made. They were replaced first by smaller Paleoindian points and then by a host of new varieties of even smaller points. These new point types, some of which may also have served as hafted knives, were no longer lanceolate, nor were they attached to fore-shafts for use in composite spears. Some of these points instead were side-notched to facilitate hafting on handles or spears.

Along with new point types came other changes in the Late Paleoindian tool kit, including the appearance of small stone tools called microliths, which probably were used to work cane and other raw materials in ways not done earlier, perhaps for basketry, or fiber or hide preparation. At the Nalcrest site at Lake Weohyakapka in Polk County in central Florida, literally hundreds of these microtools were found, ranging in size from 0.4 to 1.75 inches. Similar specimens have come from other late Paleoindian sites in Florida and elsewhere in the Southeast.

After 7500 B.C., even more changes appear in the archaeological record, changes so great that archaeologists use them to delineate the end of the Paleoindian culture and the beginning of the Archaic period. Again these

Late Paleoindian points. The upper left point is just under 2 inches long.

shifts are related to climatic changes—notably wetter conditions—and they are especially visible in the types of points made by the native people. The earliest Early Archaic points differ from Late Paleoindian points in that many of the former are stemmed. Late in the Early Archaic period, still more new varieties of stemmed points were being made.

The change from the late Paleoindian way of life into that of the Early Archaic culture was not abrupt. The earliest varieties of Early Archaic points are found at the same watering hole sites where late Paleoindian points are found. But all of the Early Archaic points and tools also are found in many more locations than are Paleoindian tools, reflecting how the changing climatic conditions presented the Archaic peoples with more places to live. Bones of the mammoth, horse, and bison, once the game of ancient hunters but now extinct, are never associated with Early Archaic tools.

Not only are the points different from those made by the Paleoindians; other Early Archaic tools are distinctive as well. There are more types of stone and bone tools and many larger tools, suggesting that people stayed longer at their settlements, accumulating more and larger possessions. Large stone choppers probably used for working wood suggest major building projects. Throwing sticks—well suited to hunting deer—were still in use; stick weights, socketed antler handles, and triggers all have been found. Because Early Archaic settlements are much more common on land than underwater, archaeologists have been hindered in learning about the culture of these early Floridians. At most land sites, all that is found are stone artifacts; wooden and bone artifacts are not preserved in land sites.

But any frustration with the situation experienced by investigators working on the Early Archaic was dispelled with an extraordinary archaeological discovery made in Brevard County about five miles from Cape Canaveral. The Windover Pond site was discovered in 1982 when a backhoe operator began to dig peat from a small pond. The plan was to remove the peat and fill in the pond—which had a surface area of about a quarter-acre—so that a road could be built across it. A bucketload of peat scooped from the pond included human bones. The landowners recognized the possible importance of the discovery and summoned archaeologists. It would soon become evident that the quiet, dark waters of Windover Pond held a scientific treasure of immeasurable importance. Glen Doran and David Dickel of Florida State University codirected the field research, which would result in unprecedented and dramatic information on the Early Archaic people who lived around Windover Pond after 6000 B.C.

Early Archaic points. The upper left point is nearly 3 inches long.

During the time the pond was used by Native Americans, the Florida climate was slightly drier than it had been a millennium earlier, but it was still wetter than it had been during Paleoindian times. The Pleistocene epoch was long past and the groundwater level in Florida was well above what it had been. Indeed, Windover Pond had begun to hold water—and accumulate vegetative matter that became peat—by the Late Paleoindian period.

Doran and Dickel and their crew of field archaeologists and other scientists began their investigations in 1984; excavations would continue into 1986. Just as archaeologists excavating underwater sites in the Aucilla River had to adapt land techniques to work underwater, so did the FSU team have to refine standard archaeological procedures for Windover to be carefully studied and to have its secrets revealed. But Windover presented special problems. Within the layers of peat in the bottom of the pond, Early Archaic people had buried their dead. It was some of these interments that were disturbed when the backhoe began removing the peat from the pond.

The Windover peat deposits bear little resemblance to the drier peat of the bogs in Europe and the British Isles that have yielded human interments and archaeological materials. The Windover peats were wet—very, very wet. Glen Doran has likened the excavations to trying to dig chocolate mousse underwater. Ingenuity won out, however. Using well points and pumps and coffer dams, the archaeologists could keep a section of the pond dry enough for the mousse-like peat to be dug. About half the pond containing 168 burials was excavated; the remainder was saved for future generations of scientists to study.

All of the trouble was worth it, for the peat had preserved an array of human tissues and fragile artifacts never recovered before from any Florida site. Indeed, it is no exaggeration to state that the site is one of the most important found anywhere in the world. Analysis of the tissues from 91 of the burials is yielding information on human genetic diversity and change during the roughly 1,000 years that the burials were interred in the peat. Such knowledge about people who lived thousands of years ago is not available from any other known source. It is fortunate that the site was discovered at a time when multidisciplinary research has become common in archaeological projects and when scientists are successfully able to extract, preserve, and study genetic material. Space-age science is being put to use to study ancient Native Americans. All humankind will benefit from the ongoing analysis of material from the site.

Today Windover Pond is fed by rainfall and by groundwater. But during the Paleoindian period before it was utilized by humans, only rainwater or surface runoff collected in it. Water tables were too low for groundwater to have filled it. The amount of water in the pond consequently fluctuated. When water was present, water plants grew, only to die and collect in the wet bottom when the water level dropped. Over time more and more vegetation collected in the bottom, forming layers of peat. Ultimately five layers of peat were deposited, two of which accumulated after the pond was used by Early Archaic people. When excavations began, the top of the uppermost peat layer was six feet underwater. In some ways, the FSU excavation was as much an engineering feat as a scientific investigation.

Doran and Dickel found that 8,000 years ago, Early Archaic peoples began visiting the pond during intervals of low water to bury their dead relatives in the peat deposits. Each body was wrapped in fabric, which was then anchored into the pond bottom with wooden stakes, keeping the body submerged in the loosely consolidated peat. Soft tissues preserved in the peat showed that each individual had been buried within 48 hours after death. Why that particular pond was chosen and why interments were made in the peat remain mysteries.

Burials continued to be placed in the bottom of the pond on and off for more than ten centuries. Radiocarbon dates from human bones and soft tissues, wooden stakes found with burials, and the peat deposits themselves pinpoint the time of the burials to between 6000 and 5000 B.C. Use of the pond for interments then halted, probably because wetter conditions made it too difficult. After the pond was abandoned by the Early Archaic people, two more layers of peat were deposited, effectively sealing the peat strata containing the human burials.

Although interments were made over a 1,000-year period, the clustering of bodies suggests that burials actually were placed in the pond during five or six separate episodes, each of short duration. Possibly each was during a drier interval when people camped around the pond. During each of these episodes, interments were placed together, forming a cluster. The reuse of the pond over such a long time suggests that many generations of Early Archaic people continued to retain knowledge that the pond was used for human burials. The likelihood is that descendants of the same group continued to remember the purpose of the pond and to make new interments.

The probability that a single genetically related population used the pond over a millennium is exciting. Genes from individuals and groups of individuals can be compared and insights gained on genetic change over time. No other collection of related genetic material in the world spans such a long time range. The potential for learning about human evolution, hereditary health problems, and other genetic characteristics is in large part what makes the Windover Pond site such a unique treasure trove of scientific information. The people interred in Windover Pond are voices from a distant past.

In the peat, excavators also found the remains of animals and plants that either fell into the pond or were eaten. The list of animals, all probably species from the immediate vicinity, includes river otter, three species of indigenous rats, squirrel, rabbit, opossum, thrush, American coot, geese or ducks, great blue heron and other wading birds, cormorants, pied-billed grebe, alligator, five species of turtles, snakes, frogs, three other kinds of amphibians (two species of sirens and one known as the two-toed amphiuma), largemouth bass, redear sunfish, bowfin, catfish, and Florida gar. Like their Paleoindian ancestors, the Early Archaic peoples apparently made use of all the animals they could hunt, trap, collect, or fish. Among the plant remains were a prickly pear pad, probably used for food, and a gourd dipper.

Few stone artifacts were found, but those recovered did include Early Archaic–type stemmed points. Pitch was still present on the stem of one, providing an important clue to how these weapons or knives were hafted to wooden spears or handles. Among the wooden and bone artifacts were a number of wooden stakes, some with the bark removed and with fire-sharpened tips. Shark teeth and dog or wolf teeth hafted with pitch served as knives or scrapers. Still other tools were fashioned from deer antlers and deer bones as well as from the bones of manatees, birds, and panthers or bobcats. The bone and antler tools are the same types as are found at other Archaic sites: pins, points (some with barbs on them), and awls. Hollow bird bones were polished and incised, perhaps for use as pipes.

Found in the peat with the other artifacts was a well-developed and sophisticated array of cordage and fabrics. The fibers and fabrics, the earliest known from Florida, are evidence that the Early Archaic peoples, and probably their Paleoindian ancestors, were expert fiber workers. Several different twining or weaving types have been identified, made with fibers from sabal palms, saw palmettos, and other plants. One fabric is a finely woven cloth of 25 strands to the inch, perhaps used to fashion tuniclike inner garments. Other coarser and more durable fabrics also were found, as were an open-twined bag and matting.

Windover Pond tells us that the ancient people of Florida made and used numerous items that were well suited to their way of life. But by our standards it was not an easy life. Water was in short supply relative to its availability in later times, and in order to survive, people had to hunt or collect everything they ate. They had to fashion all of the tools, weapons, containers, clothing, and other items they needed to live.

In their relatively harsh world, children, who represented the continuation of life, must have had a high value. At Windover Pond more artifacts were found with child and teenage burials than with adults. Water, so important to life, may also have had special significance—significance reflected in the practice of returning the dead to a pond for final burial.

As we shall see, climatic conditions in Florida would continue to change. Just as the Paleoindians gave way to the Early Archaic peoples, so would the culture represented by the people who camped at Windover Pond evolve into the still newer ways of life of the Middle and Late Archaic cultures. And even though water no longer was in short supply, it would continue to shape the nature of human settlements in Florida.

# 2 Changes in the Land Bring New Lifeways

Water. It is that simple. Water was the major factor in determining where and how early Native American populations in Florida lived. Water was needed for drinking, cooking, washing, and other everyday activities. Water—fresh water and salt water—also gave life to the animals that provided food for the people. As the Early Archaic period drew to a close and Florida became wetter, fish and shellfish—some from the coasts, others from interior lakes, rivers, and wetlands—increased in importance in native diets. People continued to hunt deer and other animals, but fish, oysters, snails, mussels, water birds, water snakes, alligators, and all the other animals that live in and around water and wetlands provided the largest meat portion of the daily fare.

## The Middle Archaic Culture

The trend toward increased wetness that began during the Early Archaic period would continue throughout the Middle Archaic period, from 5000 to 3000 B.C. By the latter date climatic conditions essentially the same as those of today were present, although sea levels were still lower.

During the Middle Archaic period, human populations grew in number and settlements of a longer-term nature appeared in all areas of the state. By the onset of Late Archaic times, people were living in large numbers all along the coasts wherever estuaries provided food, and they had moved in equally large numbers into the St. Johns River valley, where freshwater marshes and the river itself provided a veritable larder. Camps became villages and distinctive ways of life developed in specific localities. As we shall see in subsequent chapters, a few of these Archaic cultural traditions can be traced through time into the colonial period. Successful adaptations to the environment were developed and the people stuck to them for thousands of years.

As noted, Middle Archaic sites are found in a variety of locations, including, for the first time, freshwater shell middens along the St. Johns River and marine shell middens on the Atlantic lagoon. Middle Archaic peoples also lived in the Hillsborough River drainage northeast of Tampa Bay, along the southwest Florida coast where marine shell middens are found, and in south Florida locales such as Little Salt Spring in Sarasota County. In addition, Middle Archaic sites occur throughout the forests of the interior of northern Florida, where they are near water sources. One of the largest known Middle Archaic sites in that region is located on the northern side of Paynes Prairie; another large site is in St. Johns County.

The locations where Middle Archaic people chose to settle would continue to draw people over thousands of years. Native Floridians repeatedly inhabited many of the same places. Areas of extensive wetlands, such as those south of Lake George on the St. Johns River between Lake and Volusia counties, were prime locales, providing food and other resources. It is no wonder people preferred them. The large Middle Archaic sites were villages where people lived for long intervals of time, perhaps generations. Some of these villages cover several acres and contain tens of thousands of stone artifacts. They are the first true villages in Florida.

From their villages the people traveled out on hunting trips and to collect specific foods or other resources, such as quarrying stone for making tools, often establishing small camps to accomplish this. These small camps—archaeologists call them special-use sites—contain only scatters of stone artifacts and are much smaller than the village sites. Typically they contain points, knives, scrapers, and a few larger chopping or hammering tools. The nature of the camps contrasts sharply with that of the village sites, but the camps are many more in number.

Some of the quarry sites were used not only by the Middle Archaic Indians but by earlier and later people as well. Such quarries are located in places where chert can be mined relatively easily from surface outcroppings

The Bluffton site in Volusia County, one of the large Archaic shell middens on the St. Johns River. Unfortunately many of these middens, like their coastal counterparts, have been destroyed by commercial shell mining.

of limestone. At times raw stone was shaped into "blanks," which were taken back to the villages for final knapping. Other tools were chipped at the quarries. Used over many thousands of years, the most popular of the quarries, sites like the Senator Edwards and Johnson Lake sites in Marion County and site 8Le484 in Leon County, are quite large, rivaling village sites in extent.

A few Middle Archaic cave sites have been found in Marion County. The assortment of points and other tools and the bones of animals excavated from one cave indicate that it was a hunting camp. Deer were probably killed and brought to the cave for butchering and, perhaps, hide tanning, using the many scraping tools archaeologists found there.

As was true of the Early Archaic culture, the Middle Archaic culture features the appearance of new types of distinctive stone points. All tend to have broad blades and to be stemmed; again some may have functioned as hafted-knife blades. The most distinctive is the Newnans point, which is found at Middle Archaic sites throughout Florida. Middle Archaic points are much more common in Florida than are the points of the Paleoindian and Early Archaic people, reflecting the much larger populations of the Middle Archaic period.

Tools (other than points) collected from Middle Archaic villages include the same general types of stone and bone artifacts as found in the Early Archaic culture but in greater variety. In addition there are more larger tools, choppers and large scrapers, perhaps used for woodworking. Villages meant that more permanent structures for living and storage were

Middle Archaic Newnans points. The upper left point is 3 ³/₄ inches long.

needed; shaping trees into posts and timbers would have required such large tools. Sandstone hones, drills, and hammers also may have been used in woodworking, perhaps in making the many objects that the villagers would have needed for everyday life.

One village site suggests that specialized activities were being carried out by its inhabitants. The site (8Al356), on the south side of Newnans Lake just north of Paynes Prairie in Alachua County, was excavated in the 1960s. Like other large village sites, it covers several acres. Along with Newnan's points, archaeologists recovered hundreds of stone artifacts associated with the making of blades. Chert cores were first prepared and shaped and then long, narrow, thin blades were struck from them. These blades have very sharp edges and would have made excellent cutting tools.

Similar blades have been found at other Middle Archaic sites but never in the quantities present at site 8Al356. What were the blades used for? Unfortunately, acid soil conditions at the site have long since destroyed any animal bones or other perishable evidence that might give us a clue. Perhaps the points and blades were used to hunt and butcher animals that roamed the nearby Paynes Prairie. But what herd animals would have been there? It is more likely that the prairie was a lake and that fish were cleaned and filleted at the site.

Another specialized Middle Archaic site, perhaps not a village but a special-use encampment, was excavated on Useppa Island in Lee County. Today an island, the locality was most likely connected to the mainland when people went there to collect whelk shells from an arm of the Gulf of Mexico that extended near the present coastline, perhaps part of the Peace River estuary. Various species of whelks were collected and their outer shells removed, leaving the central spiral columellae. The columellae, which can be used as drills or awls or for other purposes, may not have been the final products. They instead may have been blanks for shell beads that were cut and shaped from the columellae and then taken to villages located elsewhere. Some may have been used for trade. Site 8Al356 and the Useppa Island shell-working site are good evidence that the Middle Archaic Indians maintained a more settled lifestyle and engaged in a larger variety of activities than did their ancestors of before 5000 B.C.

But some old traditions and practices remained. Like their Early Archaic ancestors, Middle Archaic Indians interred their dead in ponds and wet areas. Such burials have been found at several sites in the southern half of Florida. Next to Little Salt Spring in Sarasota County, Carl Clausen discovered an as yet largely unexplored village area 15 to 30 acres in extent and dating from Middle Archaic times. Next to the village is a slough that drains into the sinkhole containing the spring itself. Human burials were placed in the wet muck in the slough bottom as well as on a ledge on the side of the sinkhole.

Bodies, extended and on their backs, were buried in shallow graves dug into the muck. Each person was laid on a bier of branches, some of which were identified as wax myrtle, and the corpse and bier were wrapped in grass. As at Windover Pond, local conditions allowed the preservation of normally perishable items. An oak digging stick sharpened on one end accompanied one person. Another individual, buried in the now inundated spring basin, was interred with a wooden tablet with a bird carved on it.

A similar pattern of burial was found at the Bay West site in Collier County, discovered when peat was being dredged from a pond. As at Little Salt Spring, a Middle Archaic village site was adjacent to the pond. Unfortunately, peat mining heavily disturbed the site before archaeologists were called in. Even so, the archaeological team headed by John Beriault and others was able to salvage important information.

Thirty-five to 40 people originally were buried in the Bay West pond, at least some of whom had been placed on leafy biers made of branches. Short, fire-sharpened wooden stakes apparently were used to help hold the bodies in their shallow underwater graves. Among the artifacts found in the muck were small wooden sticks, possibly used as bow drills for starting fires; antler tools with wooden hafts that appear to be sections of throwing sticks; throwing-stick triggers; and bone points or pins.

A third Middle Archaic pond burial site with an adjacent land site, Republic Grove, was found in Hardee County in 1968. At least 37 people were interred in the muck in the Republic Grove pond. Again, burials were associated with wooden stakes and accompanied by artifacts, including cordage and matting. Throwing-stick triggers made from antler, bone awls, a bone deflesher, scrapers made from deer scapulae, and bone pins and knives all were found, as were shark teeth, tubular stone beads, several antler ornaments, and stone tools.

Not all Middle Archaic peoples interred their dead in wet cemeteries. Excavations in the early 1960s by Ripley P. Bullen at the Tick Island site, in the St. Johns River drainage just west of Lake Woodruff in Volusia County, produced evidence that burials also were made in a shell mound. At the

## Accidental Archaeology

Archaeologists spend considerable time, effort, and money searching for and finding archaeological sites. Beginning in the late 1940s, information on each Florida site was systematically recorded on a five- by eight-inch card; each also received a number in accordance with an agreed-upon convention encompassing the entire United States. Thus site 8Al356 mentioned early in this chapter is the 356th site recorded for Alachua ("Al") County, which is in the eighth state of the 50 United States listed alphabetically.

Today Florida's site file is maintained by the Bureau of Archaeological Research in Tallahassee. The old cards have been replaced by a computerized database, which is an important source of information for anyone conducting archaeological research as well as for planners. More than 20,000 sites have been recorded on dry land and underwater.

But despite our best efforts, large areas of the state have not yet been searched for archaeological sites. And sites are found in situations where none of us would have thought to look for them, as is the case with the Archaic cemeteries as well as the Windover Pond site. Accidental discoveries continue to be an important source of information about Florida's Indians, as indicated by these three quotes from just one issue of an archaeological journal (*Florida Anthropologist* 34 [1981]:39, 59, 81):

> The Bay West Site (8CR200) was discovered as a result of dredging operations at the Bay West Nursery in February, 1980. A cypress pond was being "demucked" for the purpose of removing and dispersing the pond's fertile peat for use in the nursery when human bones were observed.

> In 1968, while attempting to expand a section of citrus grove, bulldozer and dragline operations accidentally uncovered a buried archaeological site [Republic Grove, 8HR4] within the confines of a small bayhead swamp. Grove employee Hill Lambert recovered a few fossil bones from the disturbed muck and brought them to the attention of author Mitchell E. Hope.

> It [the Gauthier site, 8BR173] was discovered by property owner, Jack Gauthier, who was digging a ditch south of his mobile home village. The dragline operator began to see [bones] roll out of his drag line bucket and got off and observed that they were human.

In 1987 the State of Florida amended Chapter 872 of the Florida Statutes to ensure that Indian remains receive the same protection and respect as those afforded other individuals. Anyone making an accidental discovery of any human remains should notify the appropriate district medical examiner and follow the procedures outlined in the law.

site 175 people were buried in a mound adjacent to extensive shell middens, some of which were certainly associated with the Middle Archaic people who lived at the site amid extensive wetlands.

As at Windover Pond, Tick Island interments were made in small clusters in discrete episodes. The burial rite began with scraping a shallow depression in the top of an existing freshwater shell midden, placing a flexed and probably fabric-wrapped body in the depression, and then covering it with sand, some of which was impregnated with charcoal. It is uncertain whether the bodies in each cluster were interred all at the same time or buried over a longer time. Later Florida Indians commonly stored bodies in a charnel house and then placed the bones of a number of individuals in a mound at the same time. At Tick Island the burial process was repeated several times, forming a mound. Later Indians living at the same site, apparently unaware that the mound contained burials, discarded their refuse on top of it.

The life of a Middle Archaic person was not always easy. One of the Tick Island individuals had been killed by a spear in the back; a Newnans point was sticking in his backbone. Two other people also had been killed with Newnans point–tipped spears. As people settled in villages and accumulated more material wealth, other people probably wanted to take it away.

The Tick Island people also suffered from treponemal infections; several showed severe cases. Their type of treponemal infection is caused by germs, a syphilis-like but nonvenereal infection similar to yaws. Others had suffered broken bones that had healed, not always well, and still others exhibited periostitis, bone inflammation probably resulting from infected wounds.

A second nonpond Middle Archaic burial ground, the Gauthier site in Brevard County, was investigated by B. Calvin Jones of the Florida Bureau of Archaeological Research. Like the other Archaic cemeteries (except Republic Grove), the Gauthier site is relatively near the coastline. The nearness of these Middle Archaic sites to the shore may indicate that the villagers choose places to live from which they could occasionally make seasonal trips to the coast to fish or gather other coastal resources, like sea turtles.

The Gauthier burials involved scraping a shallow depression in the ground surface and then laying bodies in it, at times on top of one another. Five individual clusters of burials were found. A single radiocarbon date and the types of points found at the site indicate that it was used during the late Middle Archaic culture into the early portion of the post–3000 B.C. Late Archaic period (discussed later).

It is tempting to speculate that the practice of burying people in mounds and cemeteries began toward the end of the Middle Archaic culture, coming after the wet-site burials of the Early Archaic period and the early portion of the Middle Archaic period. It also is easy to conjecture that the burial clusters present at the Windover Pond, Tick Island, and Gauthier sites each represent a kin group, relatives from a single lineage who shared a common family identity. As we shall see, the use of charnel houses and mound burial by kin groups was common to the Florida area after 500 B.C. Perhaps this practice started much earlier.

An array of artifacts was found at the Gauthier site, items such as limestone throwing-stick weights, antler triggers for throwing sticks, projectile points, other stone tools, tubular *Busycon* shell beads, tools and ornaments of bone, and shark teeth knives or scrapers.

On one person's head were two pieces of incised deer antler, each four to five inches long and with a small drilled hole. A lock of hair could have been pulled through the hole of each ornament. A raccoon baculum (penis bone) was then used to secure the hair in each hole. These might have been part of a more elaborate headdress. The person wearing these ornaments had been buried with a number of other artifacts, suggesting that the individual was someone of importance. This is the first indication from Florida of the presence of special status individuals, people who served as leaders or native priests or a combination of the two. Although such people probably existed in earlier times, their importance would have increased with settled village life and is reflected in the accoutrements they wore.

### The Late Archaic Cultures

As noted, by 3000 B.C., the start of the Late Archaic period, modern climatic conditions had arrived in Florida. The 1,000 years prior to that time had been characterized by increasing wetness, with resulting vegetation shifts, including the appearance of widespread pine and mixed pine and hardwood forests. Sea level would continue to rise, but at a much slower rate than previously.

During the period of the Late Archaic cultures wetland animals flourished, both at inland locations and in the coastal estuaries and salt marshes. Florida Indians were quick to take advantage, moving to wetland localities. The settlement trends that had begun in the Middle Archaic culture continued as human populations increased and people moved into every part of Florida where there were extensive freshwater or saltwater wetlands. Villagers lived along the Atlantic coastal lagoon in Flagler, St. Johns, Duval, and Nassau counties and within the St. Johns River valley. In both of these areas large shell middens accumulated. Smaller middens are found on the Atlantic coast just north of Cape Canaveral and south of the Cape around inlets, on estuaries at the mouths of rivers and streams, and along the coastal lagoon, today the Inland Waterway. Extensive shell middens dating from this time also are found on the Gulf of Mexico coast, especially from Tampa Bay south into the Ten Thousand Islands. Wherever there were large expanses of productive wetlands, there were people.

At these wetland locations settled village life was the rule. Although people might move to camps to hunt or to collect sea turtle eggs, acorns, or some other resource, they maintained their home villages. Across Florida the uniformity that was present among the lifeways of the Middle Archaic began to disappear as regional adaptations to specific environments took hold and discrete cultures developed. These become even more apparent after 500 B.C.

Archaeologists' recognition of these regional cultures has been facilitated by an invention of the Late Archaic peoples themselves. By 2000 B.C. or slightly earlier, the Florida Indians began making fired clay pottery. Prior to the beginning of ceramic making, containers were shaped from gourds, wood, shell, basketry, and even stone. Being able to construct vessels of clay was an extraordinary accomplishment that would present new options for the ways people cooked, stored food, and used containers in general.

One archaeologist, Bruce Smith of the Smithsonian Institution, has labeled this the "container revolution." It was such an important development that fired clay pottery appears in the artifact record for coastal South Carolina and Georgia and northeast and southwest Florida at nearly the same time. Where the process first was invented is uncertain; what is certain is that the idea spread rapidly. Precolumbian people knew a good thing when they saw it.

Late Archaic pottery contained plant fibers as temper, bulk to help hold the damp clay together and strengthen the walls. Most often these fibers were from palmetto fronds or Spanish moss. Although the earliest pottery was undecorated, geometric designs and punctations soon began to appear, inscribed in the surface of the wet clay before the pots were fired. In different areas of the state there were variations in the recipes used for tempering the clay and in the types of surface decorations used. There

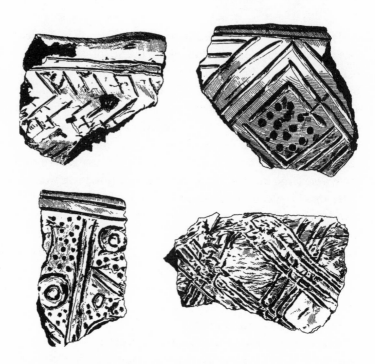

Incised and punctated fiber-tempered pottery sherds from sites in east Florida

were variations in other aspects of the Late Archaic cultures as well, which allow us to delineate and study each one separately. Let us briefly look at four regional Late Archaic cultures.

In east and central Florida, the Orange culture with its distinctive fiber-tempered pottery developed by 2000 B.C. out of the early Mount Taylor culture of the late Middle Archaic and early Late Archaic periods. Both coastal and inland sites are widespread, clustered around the many lakes of central Florida, in the St. Johns–Oklawaha River drainage, and along the coast. There are many more Orange sites present than earlier sites, indicating a continually increasing population.

Investigations by Michael Russo in northeast Florida in the Timucuan Ecological and Historic Preserve have demonstrated that these Late Archaic people were occupying coastal villages and living off the bounty of the nearby salt marshes and tidal streams. Out from the main villages were camps where people fished and collected shellfish and processed their catches.

Oysters and coquina were important sources of meat. But more significant were the other marine resources: shrimp, crabs, more than twenty

## Early Observations on a Shell Midden

The shell middens on the St. Johns River and the Atlantic coastal lagoon to the east are so extensive that at one time early observers concluded they were the result of natural phenomena rather than human activities. But that view would begin to change with the 1859 publication of Daniel Brinton's *Notes on the Floridian Peninsula,* which laid out the evidence for the coastal middens being of human origin. In 1867, Jeffries Wyman, accompanied by two friends, visited a number of freshwater middens on the St. Johns River and reached a similar conclusion. Here is an excerpt of his perceptive and scientific investigation of the Horse Landing site several miles south of Palatka:

It is three hundred feet in length, one hundred in breadth in the widest part, and rises abruptly in every direction. . . . In its general appearance the mound has the aspect of a geological deposit. . . . The upper portion of the sand on which it rests is more or less mixed with fragments of shells, and still higher are alternate layers of these, and of shells mixed with sand; it is this condition which gives the whole its stratified appearance. . . . Two explanations of this appearance are suggested: first, successive overflows of the river; second, interrupted occupation of the mound. The first seems quite improbable. . . . The second is the more probable, but in the absence of proof can stand only as a reasonable conjecture. In view of these facts the search for evidence of man's work was important and especially as the mound had the appearance of great age. The whole front . . . was therefore most carefully examined, and with the following results: First, excepting within a few inches of the surface and the vegetable mould, not a fragment of pottery was discovered; second, a few bones of the deer, more or less broken, were found, and one of them burned; those of the soft-shelled turtle, alligator, and gar-pike, as also numerous fragments of charcoal, were obtained at various depths between the top of the mound and the sand on which it rested. If to these we add an ornament made of bone . . . we have the scanty evidence . . . for the conclusion the mound was built by man. Mr. Peabody, however, made an important discovery which confirms this conclusion. He observed a piece of flint projecting from the sand just beneath . . . the lowest deposit of shells. . . . The flint . . . was evidently the result of a rude attempt at an arrow-head. We cannot, therefore, in view of all the facts resist the conclusion that the mound was of human origin. (Jeffries Wyman, *An Account of the Fresh-Water Shell-Heaps of the St. Johns River, East Florida* [Salem, Mass.: Essex Institute Press, 1968], 11–13) species of fishes, and porpoises. At coastal sites sharks and rays also were eaten, as were loons, common murres, and gannets; two sites have even produced bones of the great auk, a now extinct bird. Other animals collected for food were snakes, turtles, lizards, salamanders, sirens, and rodents. The Orange people also hunted and collected deer, bear, wildcat, otter, opossum, and rabbit; at times even dogs provided food. Like their ancestors, these native people used the animals around them to sustain themselves. They no doubt were expert at making use of the coasts and the adjacent forests.

The villagers on the St. Johns River were just as expert, harvesting pond snails in huge quantities and catching fish as well as hunting and collecting other animals. Although they lived in a freshwater environment, shellfish and fish nevertheless provided the largest amount of their meat diet, as among coastal dwellers. The successful and productive subsistence patterns in practice by the Late Archaic people of east and central Florida would continue for the next three and a half millennia to the time of the Timucua and Mayaca Indians.

Those patterns involved the use of traps, snares, fish weirs, and nets. It is certain that the people were excellent basketry makers and weavers of fibers, the latter skills passed down from at least Early Archaic times. A few of the fiber-tempered vessels still retain basketry, matting, and woven-fiber impressions on their bottoms, impressions probably unintentionally made when the pots were being shaped.

Like their ancestors, Orange villagers used the throwing stick; some spears were tipped with stone points. Throwing-stick weights made of steatite—a soft, talclike stone, the closest source of which is near Atlanta—indicate that Late Archaic people did not live in isolation but were in contact with people from far away. Trade routes provided not only goods but opportunities for the exchange of ideas as well.

Other tools associated with Orange culture sites in east and central Florida are similar to the stone, bone, and shell artifacts of earlier and later times, although marine shell tools—ax and adze bits and hammers and cups made from parts of whelk shells—appear for the first time. Shell picks and bone points, awls, and pins are common.

At the same time as the Orange culture flourished in east and central Florida, Late Archaic people also were living in northwest Florida. Small sites—probably special-use camps—are found from the coast into the interior forests, such as in the Torreya Ravines region of Gadsden and Liberty counties and around the lakes of Leon County. Larger interior sites,

Bone tools like these from the Ichetucknee River were used by Florida Indians from at least the early Archaic period into the Orange period. The upper right artifact, perhaps a fish spear made from a splintered deer bone, is 4 ¾ inches long.

probably villages, are found near wetlands at the Jim Woodruff Reservoir and in the Apalachicola River valley near the coast. The largest and most numerous sites, however, are shell middens found around Choctawhatchee Bay on the panhandle coast eastward to the Apalachicola River. Archaeologists have grouped the artifacts associated with these latter sites into the Elliott's Point complex and have recognized that the complex is related to the Poverty Point culture, the heartland of which is in the lower Mississippi River Valley.

How could that be? A glance at a map tells us why. The distance from Fort Walton Beach on the west end of Choctawhatchee Bay to New Orleans on the Mississippi River is 220 airline miles, all of which could be traveled by water. From Fort Walton Beach to Jacksonville is 295 miles, all nearly overland. Geographically and, not surprisingly, culturally, the western panhandle was closer to the Mississippi River culture(s) than it was to the cultures of the St. Johns River. As we shall see, those western ties would continue into the post–500 B.C. period.

Fiber-tempered pottery of northwest Florida is similar to its Orange counterpart, but most often it is decorated with stick impressions rather than incised designs. Because the pottery's surface motifs are different from the designs on Orange pottery, archaeologists have given the pottery a separate name, calling it Norwood. Norwood pottery is not found at the earliest Elliott's Point complex sites. As in east and central Florida, the adoption of fired clay pottery by northwest Florida Indians occurred after people already were living in villages.

Caleb Curren's investigation of the Meig's Pasture site in Okaloosa County, an Elliott's Point complex site on the coastline near a freshwater spring, revealed a horseshoe-shaped village midden 320 feet across at the open end. Large, trenchlike cooking pits were used, and cooking was aided by the use of tennis ball–sized clay balls like those found in Poverty Point sites. These were heated in a fire and then transferred to an "earth oven" or pit where their heat could bake food.

After use, the cooking ovens or pits were filled with refuse from meals, providing small time capsules of information relating to the villagers' diet. As we might expect, they dined on a variety of shellfish (more than 20 species) and fish (nearly 15 species), as well as freshwater turtles, small mammals, and deer. Plant foods included wild grapes, hickory nuts, and cabbage palm seeds.

A third area of Late Archaic settlement is the central peninsular Gulf coast. Again sites with fiber-tempered pottery—both Norwood and Orange—and slightly earlier sites without pottery are present. The name Culbreath Bayou has been suggested for this culture. Camps and small villages occur inland in the wetlands of the Hillsborough River, while large sites with shell middens are on Tampa Bay and south along the Sarasota County coast. The prime coastal locations continued to be occupied well beyond the end of the Culbreath culture, after 500 B.C.

Distinctive stemmed and corner-notched projectile points are associated with the Culbreath culture. Other artifacts include steatite ornaments,

Middle (top two rows) and Late Archaic points. The upper left specimen is 2 ³/₈ inches long.

pieces of sandstone and steatite containers, bone awls, whelk shell hammers and picks, and stone cleavers. A carnivore jaw effigy carved from slate probably was part of a mask or costume. Florida Indians made masks from animals' jaws—often wolf or panther—which were held partly in the wearer's mouth, helping the individual assume the guise of the animal.

In contrast to the Late Archaic sites in the Tampa Bay region, which have received a relatively small amount of archaeological attention, investigations south of Charlotte Harbor in Lee and Collier counties have provided us with a great deal of information. Some shell middens from this time on southern Marco Island and on nearby Horr's Island bordering Barfield Bay are 16 feet thick. As in other regions of the state, fiber-tempered pottery is found in the sites dating from after 2000 B.C. Late Archaic sites occupied prior to that time do not contain pottery.

The most extensive investigations were carried out by Alan McMichael and later by Michael Russo on Horr's Island, where the Late Archaic sites date from 3000 to 2000 B.C. Occupation ceased just as fiber-tempered pottery was first adopted, about the same time the local population apparently moved across Barfield Bay to Marco Island, where sites with fiber-tempered pottery have been found.

Russo's research demonstrated that the Late Archaic occupants of Horr's Island lived there year-round in a large village, its midden covering an area 300 by 600 yards. Within the village are numerous small hearths and post molds suggesting circular to oval houses, measuring 13 by 15 feet in diameter. From their coastal village the Late Archaic villagers had easy access to marine resources, the same resources that would sustain the later native people of the general region, such as the Calusa Indians. Russo identified 88 animal species that provided food, 74 of which are animals that live in estuaries. The two largest sources of meat were oysters and hardhead catfish.

The tool kit of the Horr's Island villagers was centered on shell tools rather than stone. Outcroppings of chert-containing limestone are not present along the Gulf coast south of Tampa Bay, and the native people turned to shell for many of their tools, although a few stone objects were used. Wooden tools no doubt also were fashioned, but as yet we have not found them preserved in Late Archaic land sites. The variety of shell tools is tremendous and whelks were a major source of raw material. Dippers and spoons were made from the outer portion of the shell; columellae were shaped into hammers and cutting tools, such as adzes and chisels; whole shells were hafted for use as hammers and picks. Clam shells were used as anvils, digging tools, scrapers, and spokeshaves. The villages also fashioned knives from thin surf clam shells.

Blocks of limestone perhaps obtained by trade or travel to sources away from the coast were used to grind the shell tools into shape. The blocks could also have been used to grind wild grass seeds, which were found in some quantity in the village and probably were a good source of plant nutrients. Several bola stones and a few chert tools were the only other stone artifacts.

One the more remarkable aspects of the Horr's Island site is the presence of four mounds built by the villagers. With the Tick Island site, these are the earliest known mounds in Florida. Excavation indicates that two of them, Mounds B and C (the mounds were labeled simply A–D), were built using shell refuse. Mound B contained a single human burial; other burials may have been made in the mound, but only a small portion of it was excavated. Mounds A and D, too, were constructed of shell, but each also contained sand mound-fill layers. Mound A, the largest, contained two burials.

The Horr's Island site, like other Late Archaic sites in east and central Florida, northwest Florida, and the central peninsular Gulf coast, make it abundantly clear that by 3000 B.C., the Indians of Florida were living in villages and undertaking large construction projects, such as mound building. Settled village life first took place in localities of extensive wetlands and resulted in the development of regionally differentiated cultures. But there simply were not enough expanses of wetlands for everyone. As populations increased, some cultures would turn toward other social and economic tools to sustain themselves and to prosper. Some would even become farmers, using agriculture to produce a portion of their diet. The story of these Florida Indians and their distinctive cultural adaptations is the focus of the chapters that follow.

# 3 St. Johns Culture of East and Central Florida

The debris left behind from eating a dozen Florida oysters on the half shell in a Brevard County coastal seafood restaurant does not amount to much. Even if 50 people each consumed a dozen on a Friday night, the resulting pile of shell would still be minimal, not even enough to fill a good-sized garbage can. But imagine thousands of people eating a dozen or so oysters nearly every day for a hundred generations. That would result in considerable amounts of debris, and the precolumbian Indians of east Florida dealt with it by piling their discarded shells in huge heaps near where they lived.

During 2,000 years the St. Johns culture people created a lot of shell piles. At one time their shell middens literally blanketed portions of the east coast from Cape Canaveral north. Other St. Johns people lived on the St. Johns and Oklawaha rivers, where shellfish—mainly freshwater snails and mussels—were an important part of their diet, and they too piled their debris in huge mounds.

The shell middens of the St. Johns culture, as well as those of the Late Archaic culture—as we saw in chapter 2—were so immense that nineteenth-century observers had a hard time believing they resulted from human activities. No wonder; take Turtle Mound near New Smyrna. Before its partial destruction during the late nineteenth and twentieth centuries, its height was estimated to be 75 feet. It was so tall that it served as a landmark for sailors.

Jeffries Wyman, a Harvard Peabody Museum archaeologist who saw some of these St. Johns–region middens firsthand in the late nineteenth century, described them:

> The shell deposits on the [St. Johns] river are entirely different as to their characteristics from the mounds of the sea coast. The last extend around the shores . . . and . . . are of gigantic proportions. They are composed exclusively of marine species. . . . The mounds on the river, on the contrary, consist exclusively of freshwater species. Anyone who for the first time views the larger ones, sometimes covering several acres . . . rising to the height of fifteen, twenty, or twenty-five feet, might well be excused for doubting that such immense quantities of small shells could have been brought together by human labor. (*Fresh-water Shell Mounds of the St. Johns River, Florida,* Peabody Academy of Science Memoir 4, Salem Mass., 1875, pp. 9, 11)

Some of the St. Johns middens were not so large, representing debris from shorter intervals of time. Other sites are quite small; the latter were fishing stations, hunting camps, or other special-use types of camps.

We can still see some of these middens today, and archaeologists have excavated in a number of them, large and small. But starting in the late nineteenth century and continuing to the present, many of the larger shell middens have been destroyed or greatly reduced in size by shell miners, who have taken the shell—often with draglines and bulldozers—to use as paving material or for other purposes. Federal and state laws now prevent the disturbance of sites that are on public lands. Unbelievable as it may sound, however, it is still legal to destroy shell middens on privately owned lands. Florida's history is literally up for grabs.

If shell middens are impressive monuments to Florida's Indian cultures, what can they tell us? Can they provide information about the St. Johns culture and the native societies of east and central Florida? They can indeed. We have learned a great deal about the St. Johns culture, which developed out of the Orange culture by 500 B.C. And small sites are just as important as large ones, for each site contains information about the activities of the native peoples, whether it be their village life, hunting excursions, or fishing. We also have learned that in the colonial period, the Mayaca Indians and many of the Timucuan tribes whose names appear in French and Spanish documents were the direct descendants of the St. Johns people. The archaeological evidence of the St. Johns culture can be traced in a direct line from the Late Archaic Orange culture into the sixteenth and seventeenth centuries.

The heritage of the Timucuan tribes and the Mayaca Indians who once ruled east and central Florida is tremendous. It also is our heritage, and it deserves better treatment than we have given it. We have not done a good job of respecting and preserving Florida's Native American past.

The St. Johns people lived wherever wetlands and forests provided shell-fish, fish, and other animals for the taking. Theirs was the land that today includes the coastal marshes and lagoon from Brevard County north to Amelia Island, the St. Johns River from west of Cocoa Beach north to Jacksonville, the Oklawaha River in Marion County, and the many lakes of central Florida in Orange, Lake, and Seminole counties. Even after more than a century of site destruction, the seasoned eye can still spot St. Johns middens or their remnants in many locales, such as on the Wekiva River or along the shores of Lake Apopka.

When we take apart these middens and analyze their contents, we quickly learn two things. First, the quantity of shell is deceptive; debris from eating a dozen mussels or oysters is much greater than the debris left after eating a dozen catfish; but in terms of dietary contribution—amount of meat—the catfish are more important; shell middens are filled with thousands and thousands of such small fish bones. And second, St. Johns people knew how to live off the land; the remains of an extremely wide range of fish, shellfish, reptile, mammal, and bird species appear in one St. Johns midden or another. If they could catch it, they did. They had the technology—from fishhooks to weirs, from bows and arrows to snares, from fire drives to deer-hunting disguises—to move food resources from the wetlands and forests into their stomachs. As a result, they and their ancestors successfully lived in Florida for thousands of years.

As important as meat to the diet of the St. Johns people were plants. They also had the know-how and technology to collect and process a wide variety of wild plants. But because plant remains are not preserved well in middens—and with many plants, little is left anyway after they have been dug up, processed, and eaten—we know much less about the nonmeat portion of these people's diet. If they were like most other precolumbian people who gathered wild foods, we would expect that fully half their calories came from plants. And plant products—especially wood—were used more than stone or bone or shell for tools, basketry, and other items employed daily.

1 northwest
2 north
3 north-central
4 east and central
5 peninsular Gulf coast
6 Caloosahatchee
7 Okeechobee Basin
8 Glades

0 ———— 100
miles

Cultural-geographical regions of the Florida Indian cultures after 500 B.C.

One exceptional site providing information on St. Johns plant use is Hontoon Island, which was excavated by Barbara Purdy of the University of Florida. Because the Hontoon Island villagers threw their trash into a wetland immediately beside where they lived, normally perishable plant parts and wood were preserved in inundated midden deposits. As with the Aucilla River Paleoindian sites, or Windover Pond, or Republic Grove, a wet site once again provides an unprecedented view of past Indian life.

Purdy's excavations produced a remarkable array of plant parts and wooden tools. Thirty separate species of preserved wood were identified along with 82 types of seeds or other plant parts. Included were what one might expect—cypress, pine, willow, ash, bay, staggerbush, oaks, elm, buttonbush, cedar, and persimmon, all local species—but several tropical woods not native to Florida were identified as well. Perhaps exotic woods washed up on the coast.

One item found in abundance was cypress wood chips, debris from fashioning dugout canoes out of cypress logs. Dugout canoes were made and used in Florida at least from Middle Archaic times; preserved examples from later times have been found in many parts of the state. Villagers living on lakes and rivers would have been expert canoe makers and paddlers. Canoe travel was likely the most common form of distance transportation. At Hontoon wood was also carved and fashioned into a variety of other articles: a canoe paddle; a red cedar bird-effigy ornament; posts; fire starters (parts of bow drills); shafts; plugs; a wedge; tool handles; small points; a bowl; throwing stick shafts; and tools that resembles tent stakes.

The list of plants used as food is as long as that of the wood species: hickory nuts, acorns, cabbage palm, may pop, wild grape, saw palmetto, huckleberry, blueberry, elderberry, blackberry, peppervine, black gum (the fruit is eaten), groundcherry, amaranth, bristlegrass, pokeweed, broomweed, smartweed/knotweed, bulrush, nut sedge, buttonbush, water shield, and spatterdock. Gourdlike squashes and bottle gourds also were represented in the wet deposits in large quantities. Rather than being used as food, they most likely were used as containers.

◇ · ◇ · ◇ · ◇ · ◇ · ◇ · ◇ · ◇ · ◇ ·

## A Recipe for Acorn Cakes

Father Escobedo, a Franciscan friar serving Timucua Indians in the late sixteenth century, recorded this culinary specialty.

> They gather large amounts of the acorn which is small and bitter and peel the hull from the meat. They grind it well and during the time they bury it in the ground the earth is warm from the heat of the sun. Since low temperature spoils the dough, they do this about noon. After the dough is taken from the earth, they sprinkle it with water so intensely hot that it cooks the dough into the form of a loaf. By the above water and earth process the acorn loaf acquires a pleasant taste. The cacique [chief] of Florida eats this dish and it is usually one of his most appreciated delicacies. It is reserved for gentlemen only, and, of course, "la gacha" is greatly relished by all. (James W. Covington and A. F. Falcones, *Pirates, Indians, and Spaniards: Father Escobedo's "La Florida"* [St. Petersburg, Fla.: Great Outdoors Publishing Co., 1973], 150–51)

◇ · ◇ · ◇ · ◇ · ◇ · ◇ · ◇ · ◇ · ◇ ·

Corn was not identified in the plant samples from the Hontoon Island St. Johns site. But that is not surprising. The Mayaca Indians who lived in the immediate area in the colonial era did not grow corn. However, corn and other plants were cultivated by the Timucua Indians, who lived north of the Mayaca, north of Lake George. Numerous sixteenth-century French and Spanish accounts describe corn, beans, peas, pumpkins, citrons, and gourds grown in fields around Timucuan villages. Evidence for precolumbian corn is preserved in cob impressions made on the surfaces of some St. Johns pottery.

One sixteenth-century French account from northeast Florida notes that there were two planting seasons for corn, one in March and one in June, while a seventeenth-century Spanish document says April was the time for sowing. Perhaps different local conditions dictated different growing seasons. Agricultural fields were cleared by first cutting down the trees and burning them; then seeds were sown. Weeds and animals, the enemies of growing plants and not-yet-ripe vegetables, were combated by hoeing and by building huts in the fields so that lookouts could be stationed there to scare away deer and other animals.

Corn was the most important of the agricultural products. Ears were harvested and either stored in cribs for later use or husked and shelled. The kernels were ground into meal with long wooden pestles and large log mortars 15 to 18 inches in diameter and two feet high. Preparing corn for eating must have been back-breaking work, most of which was done by women and girls. Cornmeal was commonly eaten in a porridge or gruel, often containing meats or other foods, and it was baked into cakes, the predecessors of our modern cornbread.

Tobacco was cultivated, both to be smoked and for use as a herb, including in various incantations and ceremonies. Use of herbs was common in Timucuan religious life, as it must also have been among the precolumbian St. Johns people.

The planting, harvesting, storing, and preparation of corn was surrounded by prayers, offerings, and rituals, as were many other aspects of native life. Religious and everyday life were intimately entwined; chiefs and religious leaders were responsible for seeing that the proper community ceremonies and festivals were carried out. But even so, individuals probably performed many rituals themselves. The Timucua Indians and their precolumbian ancestors sought to live in harmony with nature and the supernatural.

Although some of the St. Johns culture societies were farmers, agriculture was never as important in east and central Florida as it was in some other places in the southeastern United States and even in the eastern panhandle of Florida, home of the Fort Walton culture and the Apalachee Indians. Corn, beans, and squashes never were as large a part of the diet as in those other locations, such as among the precolumbian ancestors of the Creek Indians.

The reason for this lies in the nature of the Florida landscape. East and central Florida, the St. Johns region, are not blessed with fertile soils well suited to the type of slash-and-burn-agriculture practiced by the Indians who lived there. Such agriculture requires soils with natural fertility that can be replenished when fields are allowed to lie fallow. Fertility also can be assured through large-scale fertilizing, as we do today in northeast Florida, or fertility can be replenished through annual flooding that deposits new nutrients and layers of soil. Such flooding occurred in the river valleys of the interior of the Southeast, allowing the precolumbian societies of that region to produce a significant amount of their food; but this was not an option in east Florida.

Because the St. Johns people and their Timucua descendants were not intensive farmers, their economic system could not support populations as large and dense as those of the full-time farmers in the interior of the Southeast. This in turn negated the St. Johns culture's need for the higher levels of political complexity found among those inland southeastern Indian farmers. In east and central Florida the basic political entity was the village or a small group of villages, each headed by a chief who inherited his (at times, her) position by virtue of coming from the highest ranking clan or lineage. Some larger alliances of villages were formed, each led by the most powerful village chief. Such alliances most likely formed for military purposes.

Because agricultural pursuits were not as important in the St. Johns region, many of the traditions and practices—including beliefs and social and political structure—surrounding intensive agriculture either were not present or they were manifested differently than among full-time farming societies. We will return to this these points in later chapters. Differences in the importance of agriculture across the precolumbian Southeast account in large part for other cultural differences across that region.

Although the northerly St. Johns people did plant crops during the late precolumbian period, for much of their history they did not grow corn at

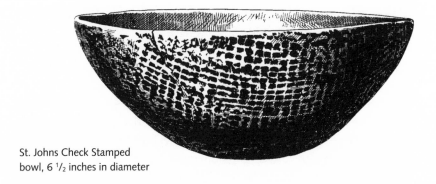

St. Johns Check Stamped
bowl, 6 ½ inches in diameter

all. They may have gardened and cultivated plants other than corn, but we still have much to learn about agriculture in east and central Florida.

Exactly when people began to grow corn in the St. Johns region is a matter of some contention. Most archaeologists argue, and I concur, that corn growing began in east Florida about A.D.750 and is correlated with changes in St. Johns pottery, especially the appearance of pottery on which surfaces have been stamped with wooden paddles carved in waffle-like checks. This check-stamped pottery remained popular in the St. Johns region into the seventeenth century. A few other archaeologists believe that maize growing was adopted by the northern St. Johns people after A.D. 1050, a time from which ceramic vessels (and copies of them) from cultures outside the St. Johns region are found in mounds and, less often, in village sites. Because some of these nonlocal ceramics are associated with farming cultures elsewhere in the Southeast, it is thought that their presence may signal the adoption of corn in east and central Florida.

What we are sure of is that farming was present in the colonial period, though it is likely corn was being grown at A.D. 750. The St. Johns region was not isolated from ideas and events elsewhere in Florida and the Southeast. Trade was widespread and the archaeological record of east and central Florida contains ample evidence of contact with many other cultures. If corn were present elsewhere in Florida at A.D. 750, it would not take long for the idea to reach east Florida.

Just as the St. Johns culture was not unchanging through time, there also are variations in its geographical reach, especially at the northern and southern extremes. This is not too puzzling, since archaeologists generally base their definitions of precolumbian cultures in large part on pottery types and decorations. Styles of pottery have wide distributions, and where two styles meet there is considerable overlap.

At the northern end of the St. Johns region, from the mouth of the St. Johns River northward into southeastern Georgia, St. Johns ceramics overlap with those of the Georgia Savannah culture. After about A.D. 1200 in this St. Marys subregion, Savannah pottery is more common than St. Johns pottery, perhaps reflecting not only a geographical overlap but a southward movement of peoples into the area. It may be no coincidence: the salt marsh–barrier island coastal environment of northeastern Florida is exactly like the natural setting of the Georgia barrier islands, home of the Savannah culture. Some archaeologists have theorized that a southward expansion of the Savannah culture introduced corn growing into the St. Johns region.

At the opposite end of the St. Johns culture area, in what archaeologists have long called the Indian River region—southern Brevard, Indian River, and St. Lucie counties—there is considerable overlap of St. Johns and south Florida ceramics. Throughout the time of the St. Johns culture, the Indian River people practiced a pattern of subsistence that focused on the Indian River itself—a coastal lagoon—and on the inland wet marshlands, braided stream system, and lakes that comprise the upper portion of the St. Johns River. From near Merritt Island south to St. Lucie Inlet, the approximate bounds of the Indian River region, the St. Johns River and its marshes are only 10–20 miles from the coast.

Like their St. Johns neighbors just south of Lake George, the Indian River people were not farmers but lived off of the wild foods they collected, caught, and hunted. In the colonial period, a portion of this region was the home of the Ais Indians.

### Villages

Thanks to historical documents and a great deal of archaeology, we can describe what the more northerly St. Johns villages were like in late precolumbian times. A typical village contained 30 houses with a total population of 200–300 people or perhaps a few more. Individual houses were rather small. They were used mainly for sleeping; most other activities took place elsewhere. Houses were circular to oval, 15 to 20 feet across, and thatched with palm fronds over wooden poles. Apparently the wall poles were bent and pulled together at the top, giving the dwellings a pointed appearance. One Spanish friar said the Timucua house resembled a pyramid.

To enter the house one stooped to pass through the low doorway. Within were low wooden benches for sleeping. Insects, always a problem around wetlands, must have been fierce; to ward them off, small smudge fires were built under the sleeping benches. A central hearth provided light and a fire for some cooking, although most cooking probably was out of doors. Foods and other items were stored in the rafters of the house.

In addition to the houses of individual families, each village or group of related villages had a large circular council house, which was the center of many ceremonial and political activities. Here people drank sacred teas, including the "black drink" brewed from the dried leaves of the yaupon holly, and the building served as the place where the village chief and council conducted business. Visitors to a village were housed in the council house and village men used it as a lodge where they lounged and fashioned bows and arrows and other items.

Apparently the size of council houses varied greatly. One is described as holding 300 people; another is said to have been large enough to hold 3,000. Within each council house was a central hearth around which there was a dance floor. A circle of interior benches was built against the interior of the outer wall; at times a second circle of benches was inside of the first. These benches are sometimes described as "cabins," suggesting that they may have had partitions of some sort. Benches were painted red, yellow, and blue and in some instances the interior walls were daubed with clay, allowed to dry, and painted with murals. The building's roof was thatched, and a large opening was left in it above the central fire for the smoke to escape and to allow in light.

Within the council house, seating was allotted by one's relative status, as described in the early seventeenth century:

In this community house . . . they have its seats placed around with great order and arrangement, with the one belonging to the principal chief being the best and highest. . . . Those of the remaining leading men follow after this seat, without there being any confusion in it, while also having seats for the remaining common people, where they seat themselves without this order or arrangement. (In John Hann, "1630 Memorial of Fray Francisco Alonso de Jesus on Spanish Florida's Missions and Natives," *The Americas* 50 [1993], p. 94)

Just as the St. Johns people knew their way around the natural environment, so were they aware of their individual places in the social fabric binding them to their relatives and fellow villagers.

## Politics and Religion

As we have seen, there are St. Johns village sites as well as smaller camp sites, special-use locations for hunting, fishing, and the like. There also are sites of another type: mounds. Sand mounds containing human burials appear in the St. Johns region by A.D. 100 or slightly earlier. Although mounds are present much earlier in east Florida, for instance at Tick Island, the St. Johns mounds are intentional constructions of sand, not shell, and they are—or were, before the modern era when many have been destroyed—quite numerous.

Why mounds? What do mounds represent and why were they built? Mounds are tied to kinship. Within the St. Johns culture each village was made up of several family clans or lineages. An individual belonged to the same clan as his or her mother. Thus in any one household, the mother and children belonged to the same clan—for instance, the Deer clan—while the father might be a Quail clan member (one could not marry a member of one's own clan). Across the village in the household where the father grew up, his mother and younger siblings also were Quail clan mem-

Published in 1591 and entitled "Burial Ceremonies for a Chief or a Priest," this engraving by Theodore de Bry says that when a Timucuan chief died, he was buried with his shell drinking cup and arrows amidst great mourning. A priest, however, was buried in his own house, which was then burned. De Bry's engravings have been widely reproduced. One of the best known sources is Stefan Lorant's *The New World: The First Pictures of America* (New York: Duell, Sloan, and Pierce, 1946).

bers, although his own father was a member of still another clan. Villages were crosscut by clan ties and people identified with both their village and their clan.

Over time as a village's population grew too large to be supported easily from local resources, several households might move to a new location, one not too far away, and found a new village. Over a long period this budding process would result in a cluster of related villages bound through historical tradition and clan affiliations.

Village ties are easy to discern; one's village is a material item made up of houses, storage facilities, and perhaps a council house. Discerning clan ties is more difficult. Shared myths and legends, symbols and paraphernalia were one way to create shared clan awareness. Anther was to build a monument, something material, like the village, that was a recognizable symbol of clan membership—in short, a mound. Interring dead members of the clan in a particular mound was a permanent symbol of clan membership, and it served to tie living members to their deceased relatives and ancestors. Mounds are symbols of clans, built and maintained by clan members.

Mounds were associated with other facilities and with clan ceremonies performed by members and led by clan elders or priests. Such individuals had special power and training and served as conduits between the living and the supernatural and between present and past clan members. Facilities associated with mounds would have included charnel houses, structures in which the bodies of deceased relatives were stored, macerated, and the bones were cleaned and stored. Often charnel houses were built atop low mounds or platforms that also were used as burial mounds. Charnel houses, essentially clan burial temples, were important material manifestations of clans, just as were mounds. Mound and charnel houses allowed deceased relatives to be remembered; after death important clan members could be venerated and their accomplishments used to inspire the living.

At certain times, perhaps on a regular schedule, stored human remains in a charnel house were removed, the charnel temple razed, and the human remains placed on the mound, where they were ritually buried within a larger mound. Often the destruction of the charnel house was by fire, and the charred remains also might be buried in the mound. The same mound might be reused as the base for another charnel house a second and even a third time. Over time a single mound could develop several construction layers and several strata containing the results of charnel house razing and deposition of human remains, a monument to the clan.

◇ · ◇ · ◇ · ◇ · ◇ · ◇ · ◇ · ◇ · ◇ ·

### A Friar Records the Death of a Timucuan Chief (1630)

As soon as the one who is ill expires, they all cry with great tender-
ness for the time of 30 days, the women with high and doleful
tone, the men in silence. . . . When the principal . . . [chief] died,
they buried some children from the common . . . people along with
his body. For this benefit, their mother and father are held and es-
teemed as leading people from then on. . . . And all the rest offered
a portion of their hair as a sign of sorrow, which they cut for this
purpose, along with the most precious ornaments that they had.
They always kept these graves separate from the rest and all on the
highest hills, distanced from the settlements. In other provinces, all
the blood relatives, both men and women, cut themselves with
sharp flints on the upper arms and thighs until they shed a great
deal of blood. And after they know that the flesh [of the deceased]
is consumed, they remove the bones and, (after being) purified at
the fire, they keep them in some small leather trunks. . . . They
maintain them in their tombs or little houses, separated from those
in which they live. And they visit them there every day and they offer them a small amount of everything that they eat. (In John H.
Hann, "1630 Memorial of Fray Francisco Alonso de Jesus on Spanish Florida's Missions and Natives," *The Americas* 50 [1993]:99)

◇ · ◇ · ◇ · ◇ · ◇ · ◇ · ◇ · ◇ · ◇ ·

Such lineage or clan-related mounds were common all through precolumbian Florida, well beyond the bounds of the St. Johns region, as were
charnel houses. Many artifacts associated with mortuary rituals were
widely traded among the Florida Indians. Just as there were changes in St.
Johns subsistence patterns over time, so were there changes in the use and
contents of mounds. At least some of those changes during the precolumbian period were related to the adoption of agriculture and an increase in
political complexity.

During the early portion of the St. Johns culture, mounds were usually
less than four feet high, although a few were as high as ten feet. Deposits of
red ocher, a mineral, were often placed in mounds as part of the burial
ritual. Because charnel houses were in use, most of the human remains in
the mounds consisted of bundles of previously cleaned bones; occasionally other forms of interments also were in use. The number of individuals
in any one mound ranged from two to 100, although most mounds contained fewer than 25 people.

After A.D. 100 the same trade networks that brought materials from outside of Florida to northern Florida and the peninsular Gulf coast (see chapter 4) also brought them to the early St. Johns people. Some of these valued goods, which must have had special significance, were ritually buried in mounds along with the remains of clan members and charnel houses. Mica and galena (an ore), copper-covered animal jaws, wooden animal-jaw effigies (also covered with copper, which preserved the wood), greenstone ax bits, quartz plumb bob–like objects, copper discs, copper cymbal-shaped ear spools, and bird-effigy elbow pipes all were placed in the mounds, along with red-painted St. Johns pottery vessels and other locally made pots as well as with columellae beads, drinking cups, tools, and pendants all made from whelk shells. Vessels brought to the region from the Deptford, Swift Creek, and Weeden Island cultures (chapter 4) also found their way into these post–A.D. 100 St. Johns mounds.

After about A.D. 1050, a time when corn was almost certainly being cultivated in the northern St. Johns area, goods and ideas from the intensive farming societies to the west and north entered the region. Some of the stronger St. Johns chiefs may have wanted to emulate the powerful chiefs of those societies. Accordingly they acquired some of the paraphernalia that those supreme chiefs used to adorn themselves as symbols of their importance. But although the Florida St. Johns chiefs might have been able to exhibit higher than normal status for a while, in the long run they could not. The economic base of their villages and the smaller size of the populations they ruled conspired against them. It took intensive agriculture to support a political system like those found among the full-time farming cultures of the Southeast, the ones archaeologists have dubbed Mississippian cultures. It was the post–A.D. 1000 Mississippian societies who were responsible for the large and elaborated sites like Lake Jackson near Tallahassee (see chapter 5), Etowah and Ocmulgee in Georgia, Moundville in Alabama, and a host of others across the Southeast.

Even though no St. Johns chiefs ever attained the power and status of their Mississippian counterparts, at several St. Johns towns, chiefs and their clans did for a time create burial tombs much grander than any seen previously in the St. Johns region. Two of the elaborate St. Johns mounds of this late period after A.D. 1000 are Shields in Duval County and Mt. Royal in Putnam County just north of Lake George. Both were excavated by Philadelphia archaeologist Clarence B. Moore in the late nineteenth century and both resemble Mississippian mounds in some ways.

Shields Mound, the largest of the St. Johns mounds, was a flat-topped, pyramidal mound with a ramp leading up one side. Rather than serving only as a monument in which human remains were interred, it also functioned as a platform on which a structure was built. Pyramidal platform mounds are common at Mississippian sites and most often served as bases for residences or temples for the elite kin group associated with the chief.

Shields, like Mississippian platform mounds, was constructed in several stages. Each constructed phase was preceded by removing the structure(s) on the mound, adding a new layer of earth, and then rebuilding the temples or houses on top. After its final layer was added, the base of Shields Mound had grown to 190 feet on a side, no small mound by Florida standards. During the construction phases, the remains of about 150 people were interred in the mound, perhaps members of the chief's clan. Apparently the mound combined new ideas about platform mounds for chiefly temples and houses with older ideas concerning charnel houses and mound burial.

The grandest of the late precolumbian St. Johns culture mounds, in terms of its contents, is Mt. Royal, whose chief managed to garner great power and wealth around A.D. 1050. Perhaps the location of the Mt. Royal village on the middle reaches of the St. Johns River allowed the villagers and their chief(s) to control trade between north and south Florida. In his excavations here, Moore found numerous exotic artifacts, some displaying symbols associated with the social, political, and religious institutions of Mississippian chiefs. These artifacts and motifs are so uniform across the Southeast that archaeologists have named the assemblage the Southeastern Ceremonial Complex.

Built in several stages, the mound was capped with a red ocher–impregnated sand stratum, effectively burying the mound and the human interments in it. At 15 feet high and 160 feet in diameter, this mound seems to have been a burial monument for the chiefly lineage or clan rather than a platform for buildings. Within it were an array of highly valued copper artifacts. One spectacular copper plate, measuring 10½ inches high and probably worn on the chest of a chief, was inscribed with a forked eye design, a motif common in the Southeastern Ceremonial Complex. Copper beads, ear spools, and pieces of scrap also were found, along with whelk drinking cups, greenstone ax bits and ceremonial maces, ceramic biconical tubes, and numerous fired-clay vessels in unique shapes. The latter probably were used for brewing and drinking black drink or other ceremonial teas.

The copper plate from the Mt. Royal site. It is inscribed with forked eyes, a Southeastern Ceremonial Complex motif.

Another feature of the Mt. Royal site is a ceremonial causeway leading 820 yards from the mound to a small lake. The causeway, 12 to 25 feet across, was built by scraping up soil from the ground surface and piling it on both sides, forming parallel ridges, each nearly 3 feet high and as much as 12 feet wide. How the causeway was used is uncertain.

A similar causeway can be seen on Drayton Island near Mt. Royal, the probable location of the Timucuan town of Edelano noted in French documents in the 1560s. That earthwork is described as 300 paces long and 50 paces wide, with huge trees on both sides, their branches intertwined overhead. Still a third causeway is mentioned in those same documents as being at the main village of the Timucuan chief named Outina. That village has not been found, but it is believed to have been near Lake Grandin in Putnam County.

In the villages and mounds of east Florida we can begin to understand the relationships among social status, subsistence, and the waxing and waning of chiefly power. In the chapter that follows we see that many of the same themes were present in other Florida Indian cultures.

# 4    Cultures of Northern Florida

As we have seen, east and central Florida were home to the St. Johns culture, whose history can be traced from the Late Archaic Orange culture to Timucua and Mayaca Indians of the colonial period. Over time new ideas brought changes to the St. Johns culture, but still its basic fabric persisted over several thousand years. Not so in northwest Florida and the northern part of the peninsula, where after 500 B.C. there was a succession of archaeologically distinct cultures. Although some basic themes persisted and were shared with the St. Johns culture, the pulse of change in precolumbian northwest and north peninsular Florida was much greater than in the eastern and central portions of the state.

Why was this? I believe that it was an accident of geography, one that brought the people of the Deptford, Santa Rosa–Swift Creek, Swift Creek, and Weeden Island cultures into contact with Indian societies living from the Mississippi River Valley across Mississippi and Alabama and into Georgia. The close proximity of the Indian cultures of northwest, north, and north-central Florida to these northern and western neighbors brought new ideas, leading to change. The geographical nearness of the panhandle to those other cultures should not be discounted. As we shall see in this chapter and the next, some of the western panhandle cultures actually represent eastward or southward extensions of Gulf coastal plain cultures outside Florida.

A natural phenomenon that helps to account for the pace of change across northern Florida is the presence of what in precolumbian times was the equivalent of an interstate highway leading from Georgia and Alabama down into the panhandle: the Chattahoochee-Flint-Apalachicola river system. Although the St. Johns River similarly was used by precolumbian people for transportation, it essentially flowed only within the St. Johns region. In contrast, the Chattahoochee, Flint, and Apalachicola connected the Indians of northwest Florida with other Indians to the north, allowing the exchange of ideas and goods.

And that was not the only river system connecting northern Florida with other regions. The Suwannee-Withlacoochee-Alapaha drainage reaches well into Georgia from Florida, and a number of rivers farther west in the panhandle flow southward from Alabama. Still other major river systems empty into Mobile Bay, just a short distance to the west. River highways stimulated trade and communication; trade and communication led to new developments.

One result of these developments has been that archaeologists have had to come up with a somewhat bewildering array of names for the many cultures present in northern Florida after 500 B.C. For guidance through the names I have prepared a chart, which needs a few geographical definitions. Northwest Florida, also known as the panhandle, is that region west of the Aucilla River (see the map on p. 41). It is divided into eastern and western portions by the Apalachicola River. On the opposite side of the Aucilla River is north peninsular Florida, the southern boundary of which is about the Marion-Lake county line; to the south is central Florida and the lake district, part of the St. Johns region. North peninsular Florida is divided by the Santa Fe River into two smaller areas: north and north-central. At times I will use the term *northern Florida* to refer to both northwest and north peninsular Florida.

Armed with the chart and these geographical terms, we are faced with a somewhat daunting task, tracing cultural evolution from the Deptford culture at 500 B.C. to the post–A.D. 600 to 750 farming cultures of northern Florida. The best place to start is at the end of the Late Archaic period, when the coastal populations along the Gulf coast from Cedar Key around to the western panhandle abandoned their old way of making pottery and adopted new techniques.

Post–500 B.C. Native cultures of northern Florida

| | NORTHWEST/PANHANDLE | | NORTH PENINSULAR | |
| | Western | Eastern | North | North-central |
| --- | --- | --- | --- | --- |
| A.D. 1250 | Pensacola | Fort Walton | | |
| A.D. 1000 | Fort Walton | Fort Walton | | |
| A.D. 750 | Weeden Island II | Wakulla | Suwannee Valley | |
| A.D. 600 | | | | Alachua |
| A.D. 300 | Weeden Island I | Weeden Island I | McKeithen Weeden Island | |
| A.D. 100 | Santa Rosa– Swift Creek | Swift Creek | | Cades Pond |
| 500 B.C. | Deptford | Deptford | Deptford | Deptford |

No longer were vegetable fibers used for temper, nor were pots shaped by hand molding. Pottery vessels now were tempered with quartz sand, and they were built by coiling and malleating. "Snakes" of tempered clay were rolled out, then placed one atop another to shape the vessel walls. As coils were added they were compressed and compacted by the use of wooden or clay paddles and small anvils. The paddles were carved with grooves or checks, which apparently allowed better compaction, resulting in a stronger finished product.

This stamped pottery and the culture associated with it are both named Deptford after an archaeological site near Savannah, Georgia, where the pottery was first described in the 1930s. The technique allowed potters to make large, deep, cylindrical-shaped vessels, which could be placed on fires or used as storage containers. Some even were made with four feet, which allowed them to stand. After 500 B.C. the use of sand grains as temper and the coiling method of making pots was quickly adopted all across Florida, although each culture would have its own particular styles of surface treatments.

At first glance we might expect that this new invention might have revolutionized Deptford society. But if it did, the outcome has thus far escaped us. When we compare the archaeological remains of the early Deptford people with those of their ancestors, the Late Archaic people, we can see few if any differences, except in the way they made pottery. It was only later in the Deptford culture that changes we can see began taking place, such things as population shifts as the number of people and settlements increased and the widespread appearance of mounds and mound ceremonialism.

There is evidence that the later Deptford peoples were in much greater contact with cultures outside Florida than their Late Archaic predecessors had been. As noted, that contact most likely was in large part responsible for the adoption of new cultural practices.

Early Deptford villages are found along the upper peninsular and northwest Gulf coasts in the same locales as Late Archaic sites. Most sites are shell middens near coastal salt marshes and tidal streams. Deptford pottery is found as far south as Tampa Bay, though it is rare south of Cedar Key. Deptford sites also are found on the Atlantic coast of South Carolina and Georgia, down to northeastern Florida, where again they are in coastal

◇  ·  ◇  ·  ◇  ·  ◇  ·  ◇  ·  ◇  ·  ◇  ·  ◇  ·  ◇  ·

### Deptford Houses

As a young archaeologist I excavated several Deptford sites on Cumberland Island, Georgia. At the time the island had not yet been designated a national seashore and I and my crew worked hard, copying the Deptford people by fishing and collecting clams, oysters, and crabs. It was a magnificent summer.

We uncovered two Deptford houses, one a winter house and one for summer use. The one for the colder months was oval, 21 by 30 feet. Its walls were formed by placing the butt ends of posts in a trench to anchor them and then bending them over to form the roof, which was supported by a large central post. This framework was then thatched. A small doorway provided entry. One end of the house did not have a post wall; most likely hides were used. If it got too smoky or warm, the "wall" could be temporarily pulled back.

Cooking was done in a large trenchlike earth oven in the end of the house with the hide wall. This "kitchen–family room" was separated from the sleeping area by a post partition. Living there could not have been too pleasant, but at least it was warm. Portions of similar houses have been found in Florida Deptford sites.

In the warmer—sometimes extremely hot—months an open, pavilion-like house, 20 by 13 feet, was used for sleeping. Other activities, such as cooking, took place nearby in the open. Widely spaced support posts held up the roof, which probably was thatched.

◇  ·  ◇  ·  ◇  ·  ◇  ·  ◇  ·  ◇  ·  ◇  ·  ◇  ·  ◇  ·

settings near saltwater environments and adjacent forests. In these coastal settings, Deptford people lived in small villages composed of five to ten families who made their living by fishing and taking shellfish and other animals from the estuaries and by collecting wild plants and hunting in the mixed hardwood and pine forests adjacent to the coast.

The growth of burial mound ceremonialism—further described later—reflects greater complexity in social and political organization as villages grew and small groups budded off to found new ones. Social ties to territories, villages, clusters of villages, and clans and lineages became even more important, as they did in the St. Johns region. The expanding populations of later Deptford times, hindered by a lack of available prime coastal locales for their economic endeavors, began to look to the interior for places to found new villages.

All across the Gulf Deptford region between A.D. 1 and A.D. 250, changes began to take place. New cultures developed as outside influences reached Florida, mound ceremonialism became more elaborate, trade with people beyond Florida's borders increased, and villages moved from coastal to inland locations. West of the Apalachicola River in the panhandle, Deptford developed into the Santa Rosa–Swift Creek culture, heavily influenced by the cultures to the north and west. Other influences from the Chattahoochee River drainage and central Georgia flowed southward into the eastern panhandle, resulting in the appearance of the Swift Creek culture. In north Florida, Deptford people moved inland, adapted to the forest and lake environments of Madison, Suwannee, Columbia, and Hamilton counties, and quickly evolved into the McKeithen Weeden Island culture, even as other Weeden Island cultures were developing out of the Santa Rosa–Swift Creek and Swift Creek cultures along the panhandle coast and in its interior. Still other Deptford people settled in the wetlands of north-central Florida. By A.D. 100 those latter villagers had developed into the Cades Pond culture, related to the Weeden Island culture. All across northern Florida the landscape—both coastal and inland—was dotted with villages, campsites, and mounds. Extraordinary cultural transformations were taking place.

In the western panhandle, the vast majority of known Santa Rosa–Swift Creek village sites and mounds are clustered around the coastal estuaries, as were the villages of the Late Archaic and Deptford cultures. St. Andrews Bay, Choctawhatchee Bay, Santa Rosa Sound, and Pensacola Bay continued to be heavily utilized. Much less of an interior movement occurred because the interior of that portion of northwest Florida does not offer extensive wetland resources for settlement.

Circular shell middens, many associated with burial mounds, mark the locations of Santa Rosa–Swift Creek villages, many of which were larger than those of the Deptford culture. With larger populations and the same amount of coastal estuary for settlement, the Santa Rosa–Swift Creek people must have faced greater competition for resources and an increase in territoriality. Within a single village or in a group of related villages, leaders—priests or village headmen—would have coordinated communitywide activities and ceremonies viewed as necessary for the well-being of the group. These endeavors would have reinforced village ties.

To the east, in the eastern panhandle, the Swift Creek people were not hindered as much by a lack of suitable territory for their villages. The interior of Jefferson, Leon, Gadsden and other counties offer extensive lakes, not to mention the Apalachicola River system. As a result, villages were established in significant numbers in the interior forests and river valleys. Swift Creek people also moved westward; sometimes their sites are found atop those of Santa Rosa–Swift Creek villagers.

Coastal Swift Creek villages were both directly on coastal estuaries and back from the salt marshes in hardwood forests, sometimes several miles from the Gulf. Interior villages, especially in the Tallahassee Red Hills region and the Apalachicola River valley, are in locales of fertile soils, leading some archaeologists to surmise that the Swift Creek people were gardeners. But as yet we have not found evidence of plant cultivation. Both inland and coastal village middens are circular or horseshoe shaped; linear coastal shell middens may have been fishing stations.

Other special-use sites are found inland, some well outside the region of the Swift Creek villages, suggesting that hunters or other small groups traveled large distances to find what they were looking for. Camps have been found as far away as Columbia and Alachua counties, and a Swift Creek shell midden is known from northeast Florida, perhaps representing a short-term expansion of Georgia Swift Creek people into that area.

At Swift Creek villages archaeologists find a much greater array of stone and bone tools than are found at earlier Deptford sites. Most distinctive is the Swift Creek pottery, the surfaces of which were stamped with intricate stylized designs. Also distinctive (in Florida) to the Swift Creek culture are baked-clay female figurines, all bare-breasted females wearing skirts with high, wide sashes around the waist. Similar figurines have been found at sites outside Florida associated with Hopewell-related cultures, signaling widespread shared beliefs across the Southeast and Midwest, perhaps beliefs related to fertility.

After about A.D. 250, Weeden Island cultures began to appear all across northern Florida, and in most regions—the Cades Pond area being an exception—styles of Weeden Island pottery decorated with incising and punctation began to replace some of the early complicated stamped motifs; the latter, however, still remained popular and a part of the Weeden Island assemblage until about A.D. 750.

Everywhere there were Santa Rosa–Swift Creek and Swift Creek sites west of the Aucilla River, there would be Weeden Island villages, camps, and mounds. Weeden Island–related people also occupied large villages in north (McKeithen Weeden Island culture) and north-central (Cades Pond culture) Florida, emerging out of the much smaller Deptford populations who had settled both areas. Along the peninsular Gulf coast, Weeden Island–related cultures extended down to Tampa Bay (see chapter 6).

These various Weeden Island cultures had somewhat distinctive economic adaptations to their specific environments even while sharing many similar beliefs. Differing local economic practices are reflected in artifact assemblages, including village pottery. For instance, ceramics found in villages in coastal sites differ from those in inland villages in northwest and north Florida, which in turn are different from the pottery in Cades Pond villages. On the other hand, shared beliefs and practices are revealed in the similar patterns of mound burial and the types of ceremonial pottery used by these same Weeden Island regional cultures.

In coastal settings, Weeden Island sites occur in the same locations as Swift Creek and Santa Rosa–Swift Creek sites. But there are many more Weeden Island sites and many more Weeden Island mounds. Fishing camp sites also are present. In interior northwest and north Florida, sites include villages (often horseshoe shaped), villages with one mound or more, isolated mounds, and special-use sites.

In the interior, village sites tend to occur in clusters. It is believed that each cluster was a community sharing social and ceremonial ties, including mound building. Occasionally one of the villages or perhaps a clan or lineage within a village became more important by being more successful in economic activities, trade, and the like. Their exhibition and sharing of this temporary wealth through feasts and other activities raised their status and, for a time, the status of the whole village. Such villages became centers of intervillage rituals, including mound building and other ceremonies.

Within a region, such a center stood out, allowing its people and leaders of its major families or clans to garner attention and more status. These centers appear in the archaeological record as villages with multiple mounds, like the McKeithen site described later in this chapter. Village centers probably grew and budded off new settlements, which gloried in the status of the parental village.

But sustaining this status was difficult, and the importance of mound centers and their leaders rose only to fall. The early Weeden Island villagers did not grow corn, either inland or on the coast. They were not farmers; some gardening may have been practiced, though that remains to be demonstrated with archaeological evidence. As we saw in the St. Johns region, people living almost entirely from wild foods could not sustain for long the overcollection of food that allowed them to feast their neighbors. The budding off of new villages, even if it reduced population in the parent village, could only have aggravated the situation by increasing pressure on nearby resources.

Eventually each center suffered a downfall, a loss of status. Community ceremonies moved elsewhere; the exchange of items that brought wealth and status ceased. All that remained were the mounds built in the village heyday and the articles of wealth or status that had been buried in the mound or broken and lost in the settlement. What once had been notable passed into history. This cycle of growth, expansion, and decline probably occurred many times over within every one of the Weeden Island cultures.

One Weeden Island culture in which we can clearly see growth and expansion, though perhaps of a different kind, is Cades Pond in north-central Florida. Just after A.D. 1, Deptford people began moving into Alachua County to take advantage of the extensive wetlands in the vicinity of Paynes Prairie and northern Orange Lake. The earliest villages contain both Deptford and Cades Pond pottery. Two of the earliest villages are each associated with a small sand burial mound enclosed within an earthen embankment.

These early settlements were extraordinarily successful and soon new villages budded off the old ones. Some daughter villages were started near the parental village, while others moved farther away to begin new communities of affiliated villages, such as in wetland localities in eastern Putnam and Clay counties on the east side of Lake Lochloosa.

◇ · ◇ · ◇ · ◇ · ◇ · ◇ · ◇ · ◇ · ◇

**A Cades Pond Menu**

In 1971 the University of Florida investigated the Melton village site on the north side of Paynes Prairie. As a graduate student visiting the project, I remember peering into excavated holes and marveling at the Cades Pond villagers' refuse. Local soil conditions had provided exquisite preservation of the bones of the animals they had captured in the wetlands and forests around them. Here is their menu:

• hickory nuts (pignut and mockernut), pine nuts (slash and long-leaf), acorns (a variety of oaks), Chickasaw plum, wild cherry, and persimmon;

• pond snails and freshwater clams;

• gar, mudfish, gizzard shad, chain pickerel, lake chubsucker, catfish, sunfish, warmouth, largemouth bass (some in the range of 8 to 12 pounds), and speckled perch;

• white ibis, sandhill crane, coot, egret, heron (two species), bald eagle, and turkey (baby birds were especially popular);

• deer, black bear, panther, muskrat, opossum, mole, rabbits (two species), squirrels (two species), skunk, rats (two species), gray fox, red wolf, and pocket gopher;

• toads, frogs (a variety), amphiuma, greater siren, mud turtles (at least two species), musk turtles (several species), pond turtle, chicken turtle, box turtle, gopher tortoise, soft-shelled turtle, black snake, indigo snake, rat snake, mud snake, kingsnake, coachwhip, water snake, brown water snake, cottonmouth moccasin, eastern diamondback rattlesnake, and alligator;

• and from the coasts: white, mako, requiem, tiger, and hammerhead sharks and large sea turtles.

◇ · ◇ · ◇ · ◇ · ◇ · ◇ · ◇ · ◇ · ◇

Within a few hundred years there were six Cades Pond communities, each containing several related villages, abandoned older villages, and mounds. Each village cluster was situated to maximize access to wetlands. For instance, rather than being next to a single marsh and lake, communities were located between two wetland areas or among several. Site clusters were on the west side of Orange Lake near the River Styx wetlands; between Levy Lake and southwest Paynes Prairie; between Newnan's Lake and the north side of Paynes Prairie; and between east Orange Lake and Lake Lochloosa. From these locations villagers literally harvested the wetlands. Analysis of the remains of the more than 1,500 animals eaten at one village near Paynes Prairie showed that nearly 90 percent were from lakes or marshes.

Even while perfecting their efficient exploitation of the wetlands amid which they lived, the later Cades Pond villagers practiced Weeden Island ceremonialism. After about A.D. 300, their mounds contain examples of Weeden Island ceremonial pottery, as was true of other Weeden Island cultures. It is to Weeden Island ceremonialism and its development out of its Deptford and Swift Creek antecedents that we now turn.

## Mounds and Society

Trying to understand centuries-old belief systems through archaeology is a difficult—some would say hopeless—task. The evidence that can be gathered is minimal. Even mounds themselves, though reasonably intact monuments, represent only the end result of ceremonies and beliefs. And mounds are linked almost entirely to burial ritual; they tell us nothing about naming ceremonies, harvest festivals, weddings, or curing rituals. It is as though one were trying to learn about our own culture's religious life by studying only our cemeteries.

Is our attempt to learn something about the religious life of the precolumbian Indians of northern Florida futile? Not at all. Much can be learned from mounds and their contents. To illustrate the types of information that can be gathered, consider a modern Christian cemetery. Headstones exhibit religious iconography, including symbols such as crosses and doves or statues of saints. Some headstones are large and costly, others smaller and less expensive. Some are made of imported Italian marble, others of local limestone. The headstones reflect the wealth of the families of the people buried beneath them. But all the headstones are dwarfed by the large, above-ground sepulcher, a tomb for a nineteenth-century mayor and his family.

A cemetery can tell us only a little about religious beliefs, but it can relate a great deal about status, trade, and other aspects of a culture. And when we can discern patterns among many cemeteries, we can learn even more about a culture. So it is with the precolumbian mounds of northern Florida—which are not all associated with burials. We may not be able to understand the belief system of the Deptford, Swift Creek, and Weeden Island cultures, but study of mounds can provide insights into those cultures.

A precolumbian Florida Indian mound, as it appeared in the late nineteenth century

The Deptford people began to build sand mounds at the same time that the St. Johns people began to construct mounds. Mounds as family or clan monuments must be tied to the increased importance of kinship identification as populations grew and many more villages came into being.

Some of the objects found in mounds are from well beyond the Deptford region and indicate that trade routes reached into the southeastern coastal plain and beyond. For instance, rolled copper beads from one late Deptford–early Cades Pond mound near Orange Lake in Alachua County have been traced to a copper source near Lake Superior. Florida whelk shells and items made from them—cups, beads, pendants—went north in return for copper, stone, and ceramic items, some of them paraphernalia used in ceremonies that may have been similar across wide portions of the Southeast.

Dried leaves of the yaupon holly, which grows in Florida's coastal areas, may also have been traded north. As noted, the leaves were brewed into black drink, a sacred tea containing caffeine and was used as a cleansing emetic in Native American ceremonies. People drank the tea from large shell cups; the cups and leaves may have been traded together.

The taking of black drink was part of the burial ritual associated with the northern Florida native peoples from Deptford times into the time of the Weeden Island cultures (and later). Evidence has been found in a number of mounds, including one of the Deptford period in Franklin County. In the mound, shell cups and miniature sacred vessels—the latter also common in early mounds and thought to have been associated with sacred teas—had been placed on the ground surface under the mound. The containers were next to a hearth. Also next to the fire were refuse from a feast, along with an offering of wolf and panther teeth. Perhaps a ritual involving feasting and brewing and drinking teas preceded mound construction. Lighting sacred fires and drinking teas to cleanse oneself ritually and to restore well-being were aspects of nearly all native cultures of the

◇ · ◇ · ◇ · ◇ · ◇ · ◇ · ◇ · ◇ · ◇ ·

### Leading Families in Life and in Death

Trade networks brought exotic items to northern Florida, especially to the Gulf coast, to those Deptford and Swift Creek villages that were mound centers. The array of goods even from just a few such sites is impressive by any standards. It includes both ornate versions of everyday items and special paraphernalia that was probably worn by lineage priests and leaders. The families that had such wealth indeed were leading families. Items include:

- copper panpipes, rectangular plates, and ear spools;
- elongate plummets (plumb bob-shaped ornaments or weights) and double-ended plummets made from copper, stone, and shell;
- two-hole bar gorgets (neck or breast ornaments) of stone;
- shell cups and ornaments, including gorgets, disk-shaped items, and one flower-shaped ornament;
- cut carnivore teeth from panther, bear, and wolf, and shell and bone imitations of teeth; porpoise teeth; and a cut panther jaw, perhaps part of a mask;
- pottery, including miniature vessels, spherical bowls, a vessel shaped like a ram's horn, a vessel with three pouring spouts, two four-lobed pots with feet, one compound jar-shaped vessel, cylindrical jars, globular bowls, and deep conical vessels with flaring rims, some decorated with cord marking, check stamping, zoned punctations, zoned painting, or complicated stamped motifs;
- stone knives or points, bifacial knives, and sheets of mica.

◇ · ◇ · ◇ · ◇ · ◇ · ◇ · ◇ · ◇ · ◇ ·

Southeast in the postcolumbian era. No doubt their origins lie in the pre-columbian past.

Why were the cups left under the mound? Perhaps they were ritually buried to prevent reuse. Often shell cups and ceramic vessels in mounds have holes knocked in their bottoms, another way to assure that they could not be used again. Having served their purpose as sacred objects, they could not simply be tossed on the refuse heap; they were destroyed and removed from society. Today we treat worn-out American flags in similar fashion, honoring them by destroying them upon retirement from use.

Some Deptford and Swift Creek mounds contain numbers of special objects, probably reflecting the high status of the families and villagers who built the mounds and that of the people interred inside. Such mounds were associated with villages that had, for a time, garnered great prestige and status, as already described. Burying the wealth, essentially taking it out of circulation, only increased its value and the social status of the people dead and alive associated with the mound. Paupers get pine boxes; former mayors get elaborate tombs adorned with an array of symbols, imported marble, and built-in metal flower urns. So it was in precolum-bian Florida.

As Weeden Island cultures were developing across northern Florida af-ter about A.D. 250 or 300, the trade routes that had brought such quantities of exotic goods to the Deptford and Swift Creek societies were breaking down. Such items are much rarer in Weeden Island mounds. The use of charnel houses—in some cases, charnel mounds—became more common and, across most of the Weeden Island region, burial mounds were more patterned; the same ritual was used for placing ceremonial vessels on the side of an existing mound and then burying them as well as the entire mound under a layer of earth, forming a larger mound.

Even though Weeden Island mounds contain lesser amounts of exotic goods from beyond Florida's borders, the mounds themselves offer evi-dence of more elaborate construction and use. More effort was put into these monuments, which, by honoring the dead, gave increased prestige to their living relatives. Increasingly, one's place in society was determined by one's birth, by one's kin ties. Much energy, consequently, went into trying to raise family status. Sometimes it worked.

The McKeithen site in Columbia County was a Weeden Island village with high status from A.D. 350 to 480, a time in which the villagers or the leading lineage or family employed particularly elaborate burial ceremo-nialism, creating monuments to themselves and their importance. The site, which consists of a horseshoe-shaped village midden surrounding a central plaza, around which are three mounds (A, B, and C), displays many elements found in other Weeden Island sites, though in more complex form.

Mound A was first built as a low rectangular platform less than two feet high. A screen of posts helped to demarcate a portion of the platform when bodies were allowed to macerate. The charnel portion of the mound contained numerous large and small pits in which bodies were buried before being exhumed and the bones cleaned. The use of red ocher and the lighting of small sacred fires were part of the cleaning ritual. Maceration pit locations were marked with large posts, probably carved.

The section of the mound in which pits were dug had been constructed in a special ritual involving an initiatory sacred fire and the deposition of five alternating layers of earth and organic matter. Feasting, especially on venison, took place on the mound, and the refuse—mainly deer bone—was tossed in garbage pits to one side. Bundles of exhumed and cleaned bones were taken to Mound C, also a low platform mound, located across the plaza near a freshwater stream. There the bundles were stored in a charnel house or temple built atop the low circular mound.

The presumed leader of these ceremonial activities lived in a house built on Mound B, a third low platform mound. The rectangular house was built of pine posts and had an entryway in one wall shielded by a post screen. Inside were several hearths; sleeping benches lined the walls. The house had been rebuilt at least once; several generations of leaders representing the village's leading clan or family probably used it.

The individuals who lived on Mound B used Weeden Island ceramics unlike those found anywhere else in the site. Portions of six broken oblong plates were found, several of which were decorated with a red-painted, stylized bird motif. The bird, perhaps a turkey vulture, could have been a symbol associated with bone cleaning.

But not everyone offered allegiance to one of the Mound B residents. The last person to live there—a woman or very gracile man aged between 35 and 40—met a violent end. The person was shot in the left buttock with an arrow; the arrow was broken off, leaving a stone point 10 inches long embedded in the hip bone. An infection set in, eventually killing the person after several months.

That death set in motion a whole range of actions, all connected to the cessation of the burial activities. Perhaps the person had been assassinated by someone from a rival family or village who wanted to put an end to the power of the leading family in the McKeithen village. The dead leader was placed prone, with arms up and bent at the elbows, in a shallow grave dug into the floor of the Mound B house. The hair (or a headdress) was decorated with red ocher, a piece of skull from a revered ancestor, and the leg bone of an anhinga, a bird also known as a water turkey. A ceramic head of a raptorial bird, painted red, was placed at the leader's feet.

The body was allow to lie "in state" for several days, which (presumably unintentionally) gave rodents and perhaps even a dog opportunity to gnaw it. The grave then was closed and a low post-and-earth tomb was constructed over it. Next the entire house was burned to the ground, and the ashes were scattered on and beside the Mound B platform. Then the platform, tomb, and burned house remains were buried under a mantle of

Weeden Island ceramic effigy from Mound C at the McKeithen site. Depicting a vulture and painted red, this hollow-based sculpture with triangular cutouts on its sides is 8 $1/2$ inches tall at its rim.

The McKeithen Mound C bowl with two dogs, a vulture, and a spout. At the rim, the bowl is 5 ½ inches tall.

earth. The final result was a circular mound, a monument to what once had been.

Similar ritual destruction and construction of monuments occurred at the other two McKeithen site mounds. At Mound A the post screen was pulled up and the posts were used to fuel a giant bonfire. Whole charred logs and ashes from others were scattered on top of and beside the mound before being buried under a five-foot-thick layer of earth. At Mound C the bones were removed from the charnel house and the house was burned to the ground. Clean sand was brought in and used to cover the charred remains, which were left in place. The bones—including teeth, jaws, and other bones that had fallen out of bundles—were placed on the mound.

Also placed on the mound were 17 ceramic vessels, several of which were bird effigies, including turkey vulture, quail, owl, spoonbill, and wood ibis. Some may have been vessels used for brewing sacred teas that had been used and stored in the charnel house.

Several of the effigies are better described as sculptures than as vessels. These special ceramic figures have sections cut out of their walls, helping to accent characteristics of the birds being depicted. The ceramic figures also were made with holes in their bottoms. There is speculation that they could have been placed on wooden posts, the carved peg-tops of which caused the wear apparent in the bottom holes. Perhaps the figurines adorned the tops of the Mound A grave-marker posts. A single fragment from one such vessel was found within that mound.

One final ritual was to take place at Mound C. It included building a small fire on top the mound, feasting, and drinking a cleansing sacred tea from a small bowl adorned with the heads of two dogs and a bird, probably a vulture. The tea was drunk through a spout on the bowl's lip, perhaps another bird head, if not a bird's tail. Then the bottom of the bowl was broken out and the entire mound, the human remains, and the burned charnel house were ritually buried, creating a third monument. The importance of the McKeithen village had come and gone.

The ceremonial ceramics from Mounds B and C at the McKeithen site and those found in other Weeden Island mounds across northern Florida depict animals that were important in the belief system of the native people. In addition to birds and dogs, other animals represented in ceramic art are panthers, deer, opossums, and occasionally reptiles or fish. Why these animals? Why were they and not others important as symbols? And why might sacred fires, feasting on venison, and drinking cleansing teas be included in rituals? Such questions may be unanswerable, but we can begin to address them through what is known about the belief system of southeastern Native Americans in the sixteenth, seventeenth, and eighteenth centuries, drawing on the work of Charles Hudson and other anthropologists.

To southeastern Indians, the cosmos was organized into three worlds: the Upper World, inhabited by special supernatural beings such as the sun and moon; This World, the world in which they lived, including the earth and its plants and animals; and the Under World, inhabited by monsters and ghosts. The Upper World represented order and unity—predictability. It was in opposition to the Under World, which was associated with change, uncertainty, and disorder. The sun, an Upper World being, was manifested in This World in the form of fire; sacred fires were never extinguished with water, which is of This World but associated with the Under World because water flows out of openings in the ground.

Living in This World between the Upper and Under worlds, people continually had to strive to maintain the status quo between the two. Violating certain taboos could upset the balance that existed among the worlds. Many rituals consequently included the taking of teas and other medicines intended to cleanse individuals of impurities, helping them back to a state of balance and normality and restoring stability to the worlds.

Within This World, the animals were divided into different categories: four-legged animals of the earth, the most important of which was the deer; birds, which were of the air and consequently had a special relationship to the Upper World; and other animals such as lizards, frogs, fish, and snakes, which were viewed symbolically as being associated with the Under World because they either lived in the ground below the earth's surface or in water sources that flowed from portals into the Under World.

But not all animals acted correctly; some crossed the boundaries between these folk classifications; others simply acted in peculiar fashion, distinguishing themselves from their fellow animals. Such animals were viewed as anomalous and threatening to the balance of This World, and they became the object of special attention; they became symbols featured in stories and depicted in art, including on ceramics. These symbols were displayed at ceremonies and rites of passage, whether a naming ceremony, a wedding, or a funeral. These were the animals important as symbols within the Weeden Island belief system. And it is these animals that are found in mounds, where they were associated with funerary and charnel activities.

A few examples serve as illustrations. Dogs, for instance, are wolves, but instead of roaming the forests and hunting for their food they live with humans, literally eating offal and garbage. They do not act properly; consequently they receive special attention, as symbols of impropriety. Dogs and other improper animals, such as the turkey vulture, an eater of carrion, are balanced by an animal that, far from being viewed as anomalous, is the very symbol of propriety: the deer. The deer helped to counter improper forces and return the cosmos in its normal state of balance. Venison was eaten at feasts, and deer, represented by people dressed as deer, played important roles in ceremonies.

Other symbolically anomalous animals held the role of mediators important in balancing propriety and impropriety, humans and animals, and the forces of the Upper World and the Under World. The spoonbill, an animal of the air, was one such symbol. Reddish in color, a color associated with the earth, the spoonbill wades in water and feeds in a peculiar fashion. The spoonbill has links to the Upper World (air), the Under World (water), and This World (its red color). No wonder it had importance as a mediating being. Complex? Indeed, but belief systems always are. One need only look at an *X* in our own society to begin to realize how many meanings even a simple symbol can have.

Between A.D. 600 and 750, the Weeden Island way of life would end across northern Florida. A new invention would enter the lives of the people, changing them forever. It was called corn.

# 5   The Farmers

We learned in chapter 3 that by A.D. 750, the ancestors of the Timucua Indians living in the northern portion of the St. Johns region likely were growing corn. The St. Johns people were not the only farming populations in precolumbian Florida. In northwest and north peninsular Florida, the cultivation of corn also was added to the economic systems of the regional cultures at about A.D. 750, though it may have appeared slightly earlier in north-central Florida in the Alachua culture.

The Indians of the post–A.D. 1000 Fort Walton culture in the eastern panhandle would become Florida's premier farmers. Living between the Aucilla and Apalachicola rivers, the Fort Walton villagers, some of whom were the ancestors of the Apalachee Indians, engaged in intensive, cleared-field agriculture, growing other crops as well as corn. Like the Mississippian societies farther north in the fertile river valleys of the interior Southeast, Fort Walton farmers grew a significant portion of their diet.

Agriculture is a marvelous idea; it allows a society to gain better control over its economic destiny, giving people a life of relative ease. Or does it? Most anthropologists feel that just the opposite is true. Agriculture is work; clearing fields, planting, hoeing, harvesting, and processing—all these activities require physical effort. Successful agriculture also requires knowing when to sow and when to reap; plants require rainfall but must have the right amount, not too much. Fertile soils are a must; hail or wind storms that beat down fields are to be warded off. Pests ranging in size from microbes to deer attack plants and their produce; a drought can wipe out an entire crop before it develops.

And I have not yet even mentioned the need to resolve arguments arising from disputed rights to agricultural fields and their produce. Nor has it been pointed out that producing a significant portion of one's diet always results in higher population growth. It is something of a vicious circle: farming leads to larger populations, which need to be fed, which leads to the need for greater agricultural output, which leads to larger populations.

Farming is a complex proposition, one with many variables. As we shall see, many Florida Indians never adopted agriculture. They could sustain their lifeways by fishing, gathering wild plants, hunting, and foraging for small animals. And although there were uncertainties in that life, the nonagriculturists may actually have had fewer fickle constraints to deal with than did farmers.

Controlling rain, wind, animal pests, plant diseases, soil fertility, and keeping track of the agricultural calendar all require much planning as well as the intervention of the supernatural. Allotting fields, settling disputes, and dealing with growing populations require more planning and someone to administer the system. And just when everything is going well, harvests are in, and food is stored, some other group raids the village and burns the corn cribs. Farming presents a host of political, social, and religious problems that nonagriculturists do not have to confront.

How did the precolumbian native farmers of Florida deal with this new set of problems? The same way all other farmers have done: bureaucracy. Greater bureaucracy is the hallmark of the Mississippian cultures, the farming cultures of the southeastern United States after A.D. 1000, which once stretched from eastern Oklahoma to the coastal plain of the Carolinas and from St. Louis to Tallahassee. The Fort Walton culture of the eastern panhandle represents the southernmost extension of the Mississippian way of life, a life characterized by greater social, political, and religious organization than anything seen in the eastern United States in prior times.

The type of political system found among Mississippian societies, including the Fort Walton culture, is called a chiefdom. Villages, groups of villages, and even confederations of village groups were ruled by hereditary chiefs who held life and death power over their subjects. Lesser chiefs and their subjects paid tribute to the paramount chiefs. The powerful chiefs, lesser chiefs, and their respective families—elite individuals by virtue of their family ties—ruled the societies. Priests shared in that power and many leaders might actually have been priest-chiefs.

The presence of the Mississippian societies with their large, often fortified, mound centers was well known to the Florida Indians. As we have seen, Mississippian ideas and goods certainly reached the St. Johns River. The power of those societies, especially the Fort Walton/Apalachee Indian chiefdom, was widely recognized. In the mid-sixteenth century, Indians in the southern part of the state told a shipwrecked Spaniard that the Apalachee were the greatest of the Florida Indians. Their fame, or notoriety, extended even to the lower reaches of the peninsula. We will return to the Fort Walton culture and the Apalachee Indians later in this chapter.

First, however, it is worth examining some of the other agricultural cultures of northern Florida to see why they, like their St. Johns neighbors, never became intensive agriculturists as the Fort Walton people did. The earliest farmers in Florida probably were not Florida Indians at all. At about A.D. 600, a new group of Indians began to move into north-central Florida, the region where wetlands were home to the Cades Pond Weeden Island culture. These new Indians, who have been given the name Alachua culture because most of their villages have been found in that county, apparently were people from the river valleys of southern Georgia, most likely people of the Ocmulgee culture who lived along the river of the same name. Ocmulgee pottery is similar to that of the early Alachua people, and it is thought that Georgia Indians migrated southward down the valleys leading to the Suwannee River and then into north-central Florida.

Because north Florida was home to the McKeithen Weeden Island culture, the Ocmulgee people bypassed that region, opting instead to settle just west of the Suwannee River in Levy County and to the east in Alachua County. Lands suitable for agriculture were available especially in Alachua County because the Cades Pond people were not using these lands—as we saw, their villages were clustered around the extensive wetlands from Paynes Prairie east into neighboring counties. Alachua villages, on the other hand, were founded in the oak-magnolia hardwood forests that characterize the Middle Florida Hammock Belt, a zone of many sources of fresh water and loamy, fertile soils excellent for agriculture, extending north-south through Alachua County and into Suwannee, Columbia, and Hamilton counties.

Were the Alachua people corn growers when they entered Florida? This is uncertain, but the places they selected for their villages would seem to

Alachua pottery with corncob-roughened surfaces. The upper right potsherd is about 2 inches high.

suggest that they were. And within several hundred years it was common for Alachua potters to roughen the surfaces of their ceramic bowls with dried corn cobs before firing the ware. When the first Europeans invaded Alachua lands in the sixteenth century, they found the Potano Indians living there, farmers whose ancestors were those Georgia Indians who had moved into the area nearly a millennium earlier. The Potano were one of the many Timucuan Indian groups who lived across northern Florida east of the Aucilla River, including, as we saw, in the northern portion of the St. Johns region.

Not only do Alachua site locations contrast sharply with those of the Cades Pond culture; Alachua artifacts and even the array of animals the people ate are different. With agricultural produce providing a portion of their diet, the Alachua people relied less on wetland animals for food, although they did fish and hunt, tipping their arrows with distinctive, small stone points.

With agricultural success came larger populations and the need to found new villages. As the number of villages grew the amount of territory expanded, and Alachua people filled the region, from the Santa Fe River in the north southward to Belleview in Marion County, the southern extent of the most fertile portion of the Hammock Belt. Expansion to the east also took place, and there must have been conflicts between the Alachua and the Cades Pond people. Soon after the earlier Alachua villages were founded, the Cades Pond culture disappeared, perhaps a casualty of the agricultural revolution.

Budding off of new Alachua villages resulted in site clustering. Archaeological surveys have identified a number of such clusters, each of which probably retained its own political identity. A series of forest trails connected the clusters; some of these trails are still used today, as paved roads. Site clusters were once found west of Orange Lake, north of Levy Lake, on the north-central side of Paynes Prairie, on the northwest side of Paynes Prairie, west of Newnans Lake, near the town of Rochelle, near Moon Lake in west Gainesville, near the Devil's Millhopper, near the town of Alachua, and in the Robinson Sinks locality in northwest Alachua County. The distribution of these clusters correlates with the fertile soils of the Hammock Belt.

Each of these site clusters was a small chiefdom, similar to those of the Mississippian societies but not exhibiting the full range of traits that characterized those societies. Just as was true of the St. Johns chiefdoms, Alachua populations were much smaller and their relative agricultural

Small triangular arrow points like these are common in Alachua culture sites as well as in sites representing other Florida farming cultures. The smallest is about an inch long.

output much less than those of Mississippian chiefdoms. Chiefs did inherit their positions by virtue of being born into the chiefly lineage, but the Alachua chiefs were not the omnipotent leaders of the Fort Walton and Mississippian cultures. And, as will become apparent in discussion of the Fort Walton culture, other characteristics of the Mississippian chiefdoms were not present in north-central Florida either. For instance, the large pyramidal platform mounds, so common at Mississippian villages as bases for temples and chiefly residences, were not present in the Alachua culture.

Lineage or clan burial mounds, as opposed to pyramidal platform mounds, are common in the Alachua region. One such mound contained a high percentage of females, which would be expected in a society in which lineage membership was traced through the female line and where males married outside the household and, perhaps, the village. Alachua mounds most often are located away from villages, and several mounds may be near any one village cluster.

In the first decade of the seventeenth century, four Spanish Franciscan missions were established among the Potano Indians, one in each of four village clusters. But even by that time, three generations of contact and conflict with Spaniards and the French had taken their toil and Potano Indian populations were greatly reduced from their precolumbian levels. By the second decade of the 1600s, the Potano had largely been devastated, and their lands came under the control of other Timucua Indians from north of the Santa Fe River.

Those more northerly Timucua were the colonial period descendants of the Suwannee Valley culture, which had developed out of the McKeithen

A stone hoe blade from an Alachua site near Paynes Prairie. Just under 7 inches long, the blade shows distinctive soil polishing on its large end from being used for digging.

◇ · ◇ · ◇ · ◇ · ◇ · ◇ · ◇ · ◇ · ◇

### A Potano Indian Village

When I first visited the Richardson site on the west shore of Orange Lake in 1970, I could not believe it was an archaeological site; it looked like an ordinary cow pasture. But University of Florida archaeologist John Goggin had found and excavated a portion of the site 20 years earlier. He was sure it was an early colonial period Alachua village associated with the Potano Indians. He was right.

Our excavations revealed parts of a Potano village 200 yards on a side, containing circular houses 25 feet in diameter and placed about 70 feet apart. There was room for as many as 35–40 houses arranged around a central plaza. Drying racks and storage cribs were interspersed among the houses.

Each house was constructed by anchoring wall poles two to three feet apart in the ground. Post tops were probably bent over and tied together. Then a latticework of horizontal slats was added to form a domelike skeleton that was thatched with palmetto or palm fronds. We found no evidence of summer houses.

Within the houses cooking was done in shallow hearths. Deep floor pits were lined with hides or grass and used for food storage. Sleeping and sitting platforms were built along the interior of the walls using small posts.

Anyone who has ever camped in north-central Florida has experienced firsthand a problem that plagued the Potano Indians: voracious mosquitoes. To ward off the pests, the villagers lit small smudge fires under their beds and slept in the smoke.

◇ · ◇ · ◇ · ◇ · ◇ · ◇ · ◇ · ◇ · ◇

Weeden Island culture by A.D. 750. Like the Alachua people, the Suwannee Valley villagers were farmers. And like their southern neighbors they, too, never utilized agricultural produce to the extent that the Fort Walton people did. The Suwannee Valley culture, like the St. Johns and Alachua cultures, was not a Mississippian one. Suwannee Valley society was organized in small chiefdoms, each represented by a cluster of villages like those of north-central Florida.

We can trace the Suwannee Valley culture from its McKeithen Weeden Island antecedents into the colonial era. During that interval of time two major changes took place in the Suwannee Valley culture. The first occurred just after A.D. 750, when the Weeden Island ceramic complex was replaced by that of the Suwannee Valley complex. At that same time, Weeden Island villages were abandoned, ceremonial pottery no longer was made, and people appear to have spread across the landscape, living in small hamlets and homesteads. I believe that this change represents the initial adoption of corn agriculture and an attempt by individual families to find good soils for their crops.

Many more early Suwannee Valley sites are known than Weeden Island sites, but they are smaller and many are in localities not utilized by the earlier Weeden Island people. There is variety in the ceramic assemblages across the region, suggesting social fragmentation. Mounds appear to be fewer in number and the elaborate, lineage-honoring mounds of earlier times are not present.

Then about A.D. 1250 or somewhat later—a guess, since we do not have any radiocarbon dates—the practice of maintaining dispersed settlements ended, and villages again became the primary form of settlement. Village clusters, chiefs, lineage mounds, and the use of charnel houses reappeared among the farming Suwannee Valley people. When the Hernando de Soto expedition marched though the region in the summer and early fall of 1539, there were a number of small chiefdoms, each consisting of a cluster of villages with associated mounds. The people spoke a dialect of the Timucuan language. The chiefdoms were distributed within the Hammock Belt in Suwannee, Columbia, and Hamilton counties. They also extended westward toward the Aucilla River in Madison County, where good soils are found.

As in north-central Florida, a series of trails interconnected these north Florida Timucuan groups, whom modern researchers sometimes refer to collectively as the northern Utina. Those same trails were used by the de Soto expedition and they would be used in the seventeenth century by the Spanish friars who established missions among Timucuan chiefdoms in the region.

At the same time that the Suwannee Valley culture appeared and evolved in north Florida east of the Aucilla River, similar developments were beginning west of the river in the eastern panhandle, but there the outcome would be dramatically different. In that region the Wakulla culture took hold after A.D. 750, growing out of the Weeden Island culture, just as the Suwannee Valley culture evolved out of its Weeden Island roots in north Florida. Initially the Wakulla settlement pattern mirrored that of the Suwannee Valley culture. There were fewer villages, and smaller, more numerous sites (agricultural hamlets) appeared; people also moved into localities that had been little utilized or not lived in at all during the earlier Weeden Island period.

This dispersed settlement pattern made cooperative ceremonial activities, like those of the early Weeden Island culture, less important and less popular. Indeed, the competition for the best agricultural lands probably was detrimental to such endeavors.

Wakulla burial mounds exhibit little elaboration; there are no sites displaying the complex set of charnel activities that were present earlier at the McKeithen site and other Weeden Island mound centers across northern Florida. Occasionally Wakulla people reused earlier mounds for burials rather than building new ones. As in north Florida, all these changes reflect the initial adoption of corn agriculture.

These Wakulla agricultural hamlets, such as the Torreya Ravines in Gadsden County east of the Apalachicola River, were small, consisting of five to seven households spaced around spring heads, which provided fresh water. One Torreya hamlet actually was on an earlier Weeden Island site. The Wakulla farmers may have discovered that the highly organic village middens of their predecessors provided an excellent location to grow corn.

Why did agriculture bring such abrupt changes in the nature of Wakulla settlements as well as those of the early Suwannee Valley culture? Archaeologists have surmised that in its initial phase, corn agriculture—including the selection of fields, clearing, planting, and so forth—was conducted by small family groups. Corn led to rapid exhaustion of soil fertility and families had to move frequently to find fertile soils. But these frequent settlement shifts soon used up the best locations, requiring even more moves. Some homesteads were forced into localities not utilized much in earlier times in an effort to find pockets of good soils.

More people and less prime land for slash-and-burn agriculture created problems for the Wakulla people. The solution was to begin borrowing ideas concerning more intensive and productive agricultural methods from the Mississippian cultures that were emerging to the north and northwest. Contact with those societies probably was ongoing, thanks to the rivers that connected northwest Florida and the piedmont of the interior southeastern United States. By A.D. 1000, the Wakulla culture had evolved into a very different social and political system: the Mississippian culture named Fort Walton, which would be unlike everything that had gone on previously in Florida.

## A Wakulla Farming Homestead

In 1973, I directed excavations at the Sycamore site, a ninth-century single family household in the Torreya Ravines in Gadsden County, not far from the Chattahoochee River. Notable to this day in my mind are the lush, verdant setting of the ravines and a freak Florida snow storm that chased us from the field.

The 100-by-150-foot site consisted of cold and warm weather houses (probably two of the latter); an area where refuse, including freshwater mussel shells, was dumped; shallow wells; and a rack for smoking or drying meat. The Wakulla family cultivated corn but also relied on shellfish, venison, and turtles, though their diet included a much larger array of plants and animals. Broken stone and bone tools, a slate bow-string wrist guard, red ocher pigment, a clay ear spool, and clay smoking pipes attest to some of the activities that took place.

The winter house, an oval wigwam about 18 by 27 feet, had a central hearth for cooking and warmth. Several earth ovens were inside and around the house, as were what appeared to be wells, one dug as deep as three feet to catch groundwater. In appearance the wigwam must have looked almost exactly like an eighteenth-century Siouian house in Virginia:

These [people] live in wigwams, or cabins built of bark which are made round, like an oven, to prevent any damage by hard gales of wind. They make the fire in the middle of the house and have a hole at the top of the roof right above the fire, to let out the smoke. These dwellings are as hot as stoves, where the Indians sleep and sweat all night. The floors thereof are never paved or swept, so that they have always a loose earth on them. . . . In building these fabrics, they get very long poles of pine, cedar, hickory, or any other wood that will bend; these are the thickness of the small of a man's leg, at the thickest end, which they generally strip of the bark, and warm them well in the fire, which makes them tough and fit to bend. Afterwards, they stick the thickest end of them in the ground about two yards asunder, in a circular form, the distance they design the cabin to be (which is not always round, but sometimes oval) then they bend the tops and bring them together, and bind their ends with bark of trees, that is proper for that use, as elm is, or sometimes the moss that grows on the trees, and is a yard or two long, and never rots; then they brace them with other poles to make them strong, afterwards they cover them all over with bark so that they are very warm and tight; and will keep firm against all the weathers that blow. (John Lawson in John R. Swanton, *The Indians of the Southeastern United States,* Bulletin 137, Bureau of American Ethnology, Smithsonian Institution [Washington, D.C., 1946], 410–11)

Fort Walton sites are found across northwest Florida from the Aucilla River west—both on the coast and inland—and they extend into the Chattahoochee River drainage in southeastern Alabama and southwestern Georgia. This is essentially the same distribution as that of the Wakulla culture, though Fort Walton sites are much more numerous.

Early Fort Walton mound centers are found in the Apalachicola River drainage from Bristol north to Chattahoochee. Slightly later sites range from Bristol down to the coast. Other large groups of sites are in the Marianna Lowlands west of the Apalachicola River and along the Gulf coast. But perhaps the densest distribution of sites is in the Tallahassee Red Hills region of Leon and Jefferson counties. Villages and agricultural homesteads and hamlets were centered between the Aucilla and Ochlockonee rivers, the area of arguably the best agricultural soils in the panhandle.

Fort Walton culture was divided into several large chiefdoms, the most important of which was in the Tallahassee Red Hills, home of the Apalachee Indians in the colonial period. Fort Walton chiefdoms differed from those of the Alachua and Suwannee Valley cultures in being much larger, both in geographical extent and in population. A single political entity covered a large chunk of territory; for instance, the Apalachee Indian chiefdom encompassed the entire region that today makes up Leon and Jefferson counties.

Not all Fort Walton chiefdoms were equal in political power; some localities could support denser agricultural populations than others. And the power of chiefdoms might have ebbed and flowed due to warfare or for other reasons. Chiefdoms were not static entities.

Fort Walton chiefdoms also differed from those of other contemporary Florida cultures in their hierarchical system of political organization; most had a complex bureaucracy. At the top of each chiefdom was a paramount chief and the chief's family, which may have included priests or priest-chiefs and subchiefs. Vassal to the paramount chief were other chiefs, some of whom were chiefs of individual towns while others were regional chiefs who controlled several town chiefs. *Town* may be a misnomer, since communities included not only the main village but outlying agricultural homesteads and hamlets as well. Indeed, in the Tallahassee Hills the largest portion of the population probably lived on family farms away from towns. These farmers, the ordinary people, were at the low end of the social system, below town chiefs, regional chiefs, and the paramount chief and his family.

Fort Walton pottery vessels; the upper right water bottle is 7 inches tall. Some incised and punctated decorative motifs resemble those of the Safety Harbor culture and other post–A.D. 1000 cultures of the interior of the Southeast.

This reflects another way that Fort Walton chiefdoms were different from non-Mississippian Florida chiefdoms; they had a hierarchical settlement structure that mirrored the bureaucracy. At the bottom of the settlement hierarchy were small farmsteads, each consisting of one or two houses, which dotted the landscape. Next were larger hamlet settlements with five to ten houses, again occupied by farming families. Hamlets were small community centers and most probably had a building where communal religious and governmental activities took place. The families from the outlying homesteads identified with one of these hamlets and probably attended festivities there.

Within each group of hamlets was a "town-center" with a chief and other officials to whom the farmers paid allegiance and tribute. Agricultural families may have traveled into town on special occasions to attend ceremonies, for markets, to perform mandated labor, or to deliver a share of their crops to the chief. Town-centers had plazas around which pyramidal mounds were constructed as bases for homes and temples for the governing family and officials. Within the temples, priests could perform ceremonies to assure proper rainfall and to seek the involvement of the supernatural in agricultural, military, and governmental endeavors. Town-center chiefs, especially the regional chiefs, who controlled several towns, had great power; they helped to organize trade, agriculture, and many other cultural endeavors.

But even these chiefs had to answer to the paramount chief, who resided with family members and other elite individuals at the capital, the grandest of the chiefdom's settlements. The largest of these Fort Walton capitals is the Lake Jackson site within the Tallahassee Hills chiefdom. The Lake Jackson chiefs were paid homage by their vassal chiefs who lived at town-centers around Lake Jackson, Lake Iamonia, Lake Miccosukee, and the now dry Lake Lafayette.

The Lake Jackson site is a typical Mississippian capital, home to generations of chiefs and elite families. Now a state park, this site in Leon County contains seven platform mounds used by the chief and other officials and their families. The largest mound, Mound 2, measures nearly 90 by 100 yards along its rectangular base and is 36 feet high, with a ramp on its east side. By any standards, Lake Jackson was an imposing Mississippian capital.

From Lake Jackson, the paramount chief ruled the realm, giving orders, offering supplication to supernatural beings, and collecting tribute from vassal chiefs in the form of crops, rabbit furs, bear skins, feather cloaks, and a host of other valued goods. In return the vassal chiefs' status was sustained.

The capital itself was a symbol of the ruling family's dominance and importance. Temples and mounds—shrines adorned with symbols of office and power, some containing the ancestral remains of famous past chiefs—were tangible reminders of the realities of the Fort Walton social system and the special powers of its ruling class. It was they who held the arcane knowledge necessary for the well-being and perpetuation of society and the Mississippian way of life. Lake Jackson's mounds—monuments to its elite occupants—served to validate their right to rule.

All of this bureaucracy was built on intensive farming. Corn, beans, squashes, sunflowers, and pumpkins were grown in cleared fields that adjoined homesteads, hamlets, and villages alike. Fields were carefully tended, and intercropping was practiced to retain soil fertility. Crop yields were much greater than those resulting from slash-and-burn agriculture. When the Hernando de Soto expedition marched into the territory of the Apalachee Indians in 1539, the Spaniards marveled at the agricultural bounty. In Apalachee they found agricultural production on a scale they knew from

## Fit for a Royal Family

In 1975 a friend called B. Calvin Jones, archaeologist with the Florida Bureau of Archaeological Research, to ask his advice about a piece of green metal found in the yard of his new home. Was it an Indian artifact? It was: a copper ax bit, an object rare in Florida and one that would have been highly valued by precolumbian people. Jones's subsequent detective work determined that the artifact had come from a privately owned mound at the Lake Jackson site that was being sold for fill. He arranged excavations at the mound to salvage whatever information was left. What he found was one of the greatest dry-land archaeological discoveries in Florida.

The pyramidal platform mound, 15 feet high, contained 12 construction layers, each built atop the last and each associated with a rectangular temple or dwelling used by a Fort Walton ruling family. Over the 235 years that the mound was in use, family members—adults and children—were buried in deep tombs dug down through the floors of dwellings. With them, as well as on the building floors, were the trappings of the family's importance and power, a rich array of objects they had owned in life and which were associated with their elite status.

Family members were wrapped in luxury. Tombs contained fragments of cane matting, cloth woven from plant fibers, and leather clothing and wrappings; at least one person had been laid on a pole litter.

There were magnificent objects of copper, lead, mica, anthracite, graphite, steatite, and greenstone—all exotic, status-enhancing goods obtained through trade. There were shark teeth clothing spangles; stone ax bits and maces; pearl beads; huge shell beads made from whelk columellae; shell cups, engraved gorgets, and pendants; ceramic vessels; bone hairpins inlaid with copper; a belt fastener made of galena; steatite pipes; clay elbow pipes; a clay lizard-effigy pipe; a limestone bowl; a paint palette with red ocher on it; yellow ocher; a shark-jaw knife; stone discoidals (flat, round objects, perhaps used in games); and a galena-backed mica mirror.

The amount of copper was staggering. Nine decorated copper plates displaying bird figurines were worn on breasts; pieces of others were found wrapped in cloth; there also were copper ax bits, arrow-shaped headdress spangles or ornaments, hair ornaments, small oval plates, and pendants. In life and in death, Lake Jackson's royal family surrounded themselves with wealth, power, and the symbols of their divine importance.

◇　·　◇　·　◇　·　◇　·　◇　·　◇　·　◇　·　◇　·　◇　·

A drawing of one of the copper plates excavated by B. Calvin Jones from a mound at the Lake Jackson site. The plate, 20 inches high, depicts a bird figurine—perhaps a person in costume. This tracing is of the reverse side of the plate and shows riveted sheet-copper repairs.

Europe. For that reason it was in the Apalachee Indian capital that the Spaniards chose to spend their first Florida winter.

But although the Fort Walton people depended more heavily on agricultural produce than did any other Florida culture, they, like members of their fellow Mississippian societies, also collected wild plants and hunted and fished. Along the coast Fort Walton villagers grew corn even while continuing to collect shellfish and to fish, as had Florida Indians for thousands of years.

◇ · ◇ · ◇ · ◇ · ◇ · ◇ · ◇ · ◇ · ◇ ·

### Symbols of Faith and Fertility, Power and Prominence

Within Fort Walton society, symbols reflected the importance and power of the chiefs and their families, their ties to the supernatural, and their status as a link between villagers and the powers that controlled nature. These powers were exemplified in dress and other paraphernalia, objects like those found in the Lake Jackson tombs.

Some symbols and objects, found across the Mississippian world, are associated with birds, the sky, and the Upper World. Eagles, hawks, and falcons are prominent, such as on the Lake Jackson copper plates, some of which may depict chiefs and priest-chiefs wearing bird costumes. Others, such as rattlesnakes, are symbols tied to agricultural fertility and still others to warfare. Objects and emblems are associated with chiefly powers, the hierarchy of chiefs and priest-chiefs, and the adoration of chiefly lineages.

Symbols of a different sort were important to the villagers who served these chiefly overlords. The antecedents of many of these symbols probably lie in Weeden Island beliefs, altered for applicability to a farming way of life. Scrolls, loops, and circles incised on ceramic vessels were probably mnemonic motifs reflecting beliefs about the world and cosmos. Some vessels represent animals and are adorned with modeled clay heads of eagles, woodpeckers, ducks, geese, quail, herons, owls, turkeys, vultures, snakes, lizards, alligators, frogs, foxes, otters, opossums, squirrels, dogs, bears, and panthers. All these animals likely figured in Fort Walton myths and various ceremonies.

Beliefs concerning themselves, their origins, their leaders, and the world around them rationalized the Mississippian sociopolitical system for the Fort Walton people. A symbol as simple as a scroll incised on a pottery vessel is a reflection of the importance of those beliefs in maintaining the social and political fabric of the Mississippian world.

◇ · ◇ · ◇ · ◇ · ◇ · ◇ · ◇ · ◇ · ◇ ·

Nearly a century after de Soto and his army marched almost the length of Apalachee Indian territory to winter at the capital town of Iniahica, the chain of Spanish Franciscan missions that had stretched westward from St. Augustine across the land of the Timucua would reach the Aucilla River. Within only a few years after 1633, a dozen or so missions would be established in major Apalachee towns. Soon the missions were followed by haciendas, where newcomers took advantage of Apalachee labor and know-how to grow corn and other products that were exported to St. Augustine and even to the Caribbean. Apalachee would be the breadbasket of the Spanish colony during the second half of the seventeenth century. It is no exaggeration to say that Spain's La Florida colony was built atop the Apalachee Indians and their agricultural traditions, colonial-era progeny of the Fort Walton culture.

As noted, the Fort Walton chiefdoms, especially that of the Tallahassee Hills and the Apalachee Indians, did not go unnoticed by other native societies in Florida. Contact was ongoing. How could the chiefs of the relatively small and simple Suwannee Valley chiefdoms deal with the chiefs of Lake Jackson and the outlying town-centers and the military and bureaucratic might those chiefs represented? The ancestors of the Timucua in north peninsular Florida employed two strategies. One was to pretend, to act just as prominent, to try to surround oneself with just as much pomp and paraphernalia. If the Apalachee chief was carried in a litter on the shoulders of leading citizens and if the chief's arrival was announced by people blowing whelk trumpets, then one should have a litter built and break out the trumpets. If the chief had an *iniha,* a talking chief, to relay pronouncements, then one should appoint a similar official. Timucuan chiefs borrowed liberally from their Mississippian neighbors. When appropriate, they acted as though they, too, were leaders of complex bureaucracies. In diplomacy, appearance and tact count. To be able to interact effectively with Fort Walton chiefs, other groups tried to mirror aspects of Fort Walton culture.

A second strategy employed by the Suwannee Valley Timucuan chiefs was to create more complex political systems, ones that could be sustained not on the basis of intensive agricultural production, as were the Fort Walton chiefdoms, but on the basis of diplomatic and political alliances. A chief of a small Suwannee Valley chiefdom might use diplomatic cajoling, the threat of military retribution, gifts, intermarriage, and other methods to convince the chiefs of several other small chiefdoms to join such a confederation. Instead of being able to summon only a few hundred warriors in the face of a perceived Apalachee military threat, a chief could then call up several times that number. And when negotiating, an Apalachee chief would realize that his or her Timucuan counterpart ostensibly represented not a few hundred villagers but several thousand. Confederations of small chiefdoms, though short-lived, were a way to try to counter and contain the Apalachee Indians and their political and military power.

When de Soto marched through north Florida, much of the region of the Suwannee Valley culture was confederated under several leading Timucuan chiefs, of whom the most important was Uzachile, chief of a village in Madison County near Lake Sampala. Uzachile kept a healthy distance between himself and the Aucilla River—the boundary of Apalachee territory—as a first line of defense. But if additional measures were needed to stand up to the Apalachee, he could try chiefly diplomacy. If that did not work, he next could call on his fellow chiefs, members of the confederation, to provide military support.

The threat presented by de Soto's army was handled by Chief Uzachile in exactly this same fashion: first diplomatic tact and a display of chiefly pomp and, when that failed, military action. But native military tactics could not stand up to those of the Spaniards, and the Suwannee Valley Timucua took severe losses, including the deaths of many chiefs and hundreds of warriors.

Mississippian societies also influenced the nature of precolumbian lifeways in the western panhandle. After A.D. 1000, variants of the Fort Walton culture were common west of the Apalachicola River. Numerous village sites, some with mounds, and small farming homesteads are clustered around the coastal bays and estuaries of the western panhandle. Farther west around Mobile Bay and northward up the river valleys of Alabama's coastal plain and into the piedmont were other Mississippian societies just as grand as that of the Tallahassee Hills. The influence of those Mississippian cultures outside Florida on the western panhandle increased over time. By A.D. 1200, such influences had brought about sufficient changes in the western Fort Walton archaeological assemblage for modern researchers to recognize a new culture, one named Pensacola.

The Pensacola culture of the western panhandle was divided into several chiefdoms, each probably centered on a shallow bay-estuary system, such as Choctawhatchee Bay, Pensacola Bay, and Perdido Bay. Few sites are inland, most likely due to a lack of good agricultural soils. Even the coastal soils are not well suited to intensive farming. As a result, Pensacola agriculture never developed into the Fort Walton system of intensive cleared-field farming found in the eastern panhandle. Instead, Pensacola's economic pattern seems to have depended on coastal resources, supplemented by agricultural produce.

Town-centers, each with a platform mound, were present within each Pensacola chiefdom, but the full hierarchical settlement arrangement of the eastern Fort Walton region and other inland Mississippian cultures was not. Nor is there evidence for the complex Mississippian political bureaucracies. With limited agricultural potential, the Pensacola chiefdoms, centered as they were on the coast, could only mirror aspects of the true Mississippian. The same is true of the Safety Harbor chiefdoms of the peninsular Gulf coast, described in the next chapter.

# 6   Peninsular Gulf Coast

Today in Florida there is an ongoing debate about water. Actually the problem under discussion is not so much water but the lack of it. Eventually there will not be enough fresh water to meet the demands of the people living in some of the state's urban areas. The availability of water may someday have bearing on how and where people live.

As we have seen, in the past, the accessibility or lack of water likewise had a major impact on how and where people lived in Florida. Fresh water to drink, salt water in which to fish and collect shellfish, inland marshes for harvesting a variety of fish, birds, and other animals—all were factors influencing precolumbian lives. Rising sea levels circumscribed the history of human settlements; many places once home to Florida's earliest Indians lie under the Gulf of Mexico; others are on small offshore islands, sections of the mainland now cut off by the sea.

Another region of Florida where water shaped human history was the peninsular Gulf coast from the Aucilla River south past the huge bight that is Tampa Bay to Charlotte Harbor. During the period after 500 B.C., water—fresh and salt—helped to dictate the nature of the precolumbian cultures as well as the events of the early colonial era. It was at Tampa Bay that the expeditions of the Spanish conquistadors Pánfilo de Narváez in 1528 and Hernando de Soto in 1539 would anchor their ships and come ashore.

Even today a large section of that coast, from the Big Bend region to Hernando County, is still subject to the dynamic forces of sea versus land. That battle may be ongoing, but a quick glance at a map shows convincingly that sea is ahead. The coast of Florida from Taylor County to Pasco County looks as though the Gulf has taken a huge, wide bite out of the land, which it has. Much of the former coast has been inundated. The flat coastal zone with its indented shoreline, offshore keys, salt marshes, and tidal streams is a soggy place. Most likely, nearly all of the Florida Gulf coast once appeared like that, before modern developers diked, ditched, drained, and filled in order to build St. Petersburg, Tampa, Bradenton, Sarasota, and other cities.

And the water certainly is not all salt. Between the Aucilla River and the Peace River, which empties into Charlotte Harbor, are a large number of rivers flowing into the Gulf. And for every river of large to medium size— Suwannee, Crystal, Withlacoochee, Manatee—there are two dozen or more small creeks and streams. The flat coastal topography has resulted in the formation of many freshwater wetlands (e.g., Gulf Hammock in Levy County, the Cove of the Withlacoochee in Citrus County, Chassahowitzka Swamp in Hernando County, the headwaters of the Hillsborough River), and where fresh water and salt meet, there are large expanses of estuary and marsh. The Gulf coast of Florida was indeed a place where water once reigned.

The nature of the coast and its geographical position relative to northern Florida combined to assure that the post–500 B.C. cultures of the region would be different from their neighbors to the north and east. Some ceramic assemblages are shared; others are not. Some 300 B.C. sites, for instance, fit nicely under the rubric of Deptford; others do not.

We are beginning to realize that there was great variation in the archaeological assemblages of the coastal cultures, variation tied to geographical considerations and local environments. These factors have created one large headache for modern archaeologists intent on giving names to precolumbian cultures. We have not yet been able to derive adequate explanatory taxonomies for the peninsular Gulf coast north of Charlotte Harbor, though progress has been made in the southern portion of that coastal region, from Tampa Bay south.

The headache becomes a migraine when we look not just at village artifacts but also at the contents of mounds. For instance, we can deal with the fact that Swift Creek culture sites simply do not occur on the coast south of the Aucilla River (they are not found in north peninsula Florida either). But where one runs into problems is when trying to put a name to a site like the Garden Patch mound and village complex in Dixie County. The mounds contain Weeden Island ceremonial pottery, though the mound itself differs from the patterned Weeden Island mounds of northern Florida. That is not a big taxonomic problem. The larger difficulty is trying to give a name to the culture responsible for the Garden Patch village, whose ceramic assemblage is nothing like anything found at Weeden Island sites and whose economic activities are centered on the Gulf, not on the forests and lakes of interior Florida.

That migraine becomes a psychotic episode when two more facts are considered. First, Florida's most famous precolumbian archaeological site, Crystal River in Citrus County, is located right in the middle of the what-to-call-it region. The site contained extraordinary Deptford and Weeden Island artifacts in a mound surrounded by an apronlike earthen platform, both mound and platform enclosed by an encircling embankment 270 feet across. The artifacts from this earthwork are similar to those from several panhandle sites, but the Crystal River villagers are poorly understood. The material culture present in the village does not fit snugly within our present nomenclature. Florida's most famous site remains a problem for archaeological interpretation.

The second trauma-producing fact is this. The Weeden Island culture derives its name from a site on Weedon Island in Tampa Bay, where excavations were carried out in the 1920s. In a mound at that Pinellas County site, numerous examples of Weeden Island ceremonial pottery were found. Later, the name of the island—misspelled—was given to the entire Weeden Island ceramic complex and culture. But the village site on Weedon Island excavated with the mound in the 1920s bears little resemblance to the northern Florida Weeden Island culture villages. Indeed, when that midden was excavated, the investigator associated its ceramics with south Florida cultures, not those to the north. This leaves us in the uncomfortable position of admitting that the type site for the Weeden Island culture, the site that gave the culture its name—may not be a true Weeden Island site at all!

So how is one to deal with these labeling problems? I am going to ignore them. Archaeology is not always easy or clear-cut, but I find it fun and will not let nomenclature dent that. Where we have workable names, I will use them; where we do not (especially from Pasco County north), I will hedge by using terms like *Deptford period or Weeden Island period*, focusing on time, not on exact cultural designations. What is important is the people and how they lived, not what we label them.

Let us consider first the people and cultures of the north peninsula coastal sector: from southern Pasco County to northern Taylor County is a short 155 airline miles, but given its intricate indentations, the actual coastline is more than ten times that length. No wonder there is cultural variation. Vegetation near the coast and on the adjacent mainland is largely scrub, though hardwood hammocks dot specific localities, some directly on the coast. For instance, in Taylor County and around Crystal River, there once were extensive mixed pine and hardwood forests. The rolling hills of interior Hernando County also were heavily forested in the past

Wherever there were wetlands within this coastal sector, there were people. Numerous oyster shell middens extend along the marine coast. Today they are found both on islands and on the mainland. Many more no doubt are inundated. Sites dating as recent as the Weeden Island period have been discovered by divers and dredgers off New Port Richey. The Gulf coast continues to be a dynamic environment, caused in part by fluctuations in sea level over the last 2,000 years.

Wetland locales inland, such as in the Cove of the Withlacoochee near Inverness, also are characterized by shellfish middens, though of freshwater snails. With some notable exceptions, few of these coastal and inland shell midden sites are large. Most likely, over time the rising Gulf caused people to shift their villages relatively rapidly; generations of people did not remain in one place for hundreds or thousands of years, creating the huge piles of refuse seen in east Florida.

Coastal middens containing Deptford pottery and dating between ca. 500 B.C. and A.D. 100–200 are found as far south as Cedar Key and, rarely, a bit farther down the coast. Farther south yet, in Citrus, Hernando, and Pasco counties, and sometimes to the north as well, ceramics in village middens of this time are largely undecorated and contain sand, crushed limestone, or Fuller's earth as tempering. After about A.D. 200 and continuing into late precolumbian times, sand- and limestone-tempered pottery predominates in village middens both inland and on the coast. The variation in seemingly contemporary sites only a few miles apart can be startling, suggesting that local communities were the norm, rather than larger political entities. However, in the best environmental zones—estuaries adjacent to hardwood forests—some communities took advantage of their enhanced locations to exercise more complex sociopolitical systems. As a result a few town-centers did appear, the Garden Patch site in Dixie County and the Crystal River site being two.

From the Late Archaic culture to A.D. 1000 and much later in most areas, the people of the northern peninsular Gulf coast lived by collecting wild foods and hunting and fishing. Like all other coastal people in Florida, the Indians of this section of the coast relied heavily on fish and shellfish taken from the shallow waters of the Gulf and the rivers and streams draining into it. Large-scale farming was never practiced, though corn was grown at inland locations north of Dade City in later times, especially during the post–A.D. 1000 period of the Safety Harbor culture described later in this chapter.

But not everyone lived on the coast. In inland portions of Taylor, Dixie, and Levy counties, in some cases only a few miles inland, but in forest rather than estuary settings, there are small sites related to the post–A.D. 600 Alachua culture of north-central Florida (see chapter 5). These hamlet-type settlements may represent a westward expansion of Alachua farmers from more easterly locations near the Suwannee River. Archaeologists have noted that these sites are found on pockets of better soils in the coastal region, evidence that the people who lived there may have grown crops.

Could two very different native groups be living in close proximity, each utilizing a discrete set of environments? That may well have been the case, and it is a topic for further investigations. If true, it would be another piece of evidence that political units such as chiefdoms with marked territories were not present in the coastal region. Individual communities were willing to tolerate nearby, unrelated settlements, whereas larger, more complex political entities would not have.

Inland sites with ceramic inventories like that of the coastal dwellers have been found in the giant wetland known as the Cove of the Withlacoochee, inland in Citrus County. These sites are contemporary with the Alachua sites to the north and there is speculation that after A.D. 600, some coastal people moved inland permanently and took up slash-and-burn agriculture. Numerous shell middens dot the edges of the Withlacoochee River within the Cove. Over time the people living along the river depended less on riverine resources, perhaps relying more on agricultural produce. But even so, the importance of agriculture would have been much less than in northern Florida.

Sand mounds frequently were built at or near the coastal settlements of the north peninsular Gulf coast, as they were to the south in the greater Tampa Bay region. Mound contents often differ even more than the pottery in the village middens, another sign that many small communities rather than even simple chiefdoms were the rule.

The earliest mounds are contemporary with the Deptford mounds of northern Florida; later, pre–A.D. 750 mounds are contemporary with the Weeden Island culture. Deptford period vessels and Weeden Island ceremonial wares—though not the whole range of the latter—are found in coastal mounds. But their occurrences are sporadic. Some mounds contain large amounts of Weeden Island pottery; others contain none. St. Johns–type ceramics also are found in mounds, but it is uncertain whether they were traded from east or central Florida or made locally.

Mounds appear to have been used over long intervals of time, and whether the earlier mounds were used in conjunction with charnel houses is questionable. Later Weeden Island period mounds do appear to contain a higher percentage of bundled burials, probably remains stored in a charnel house before interment. Perhaps this reflects the increased importance of lineage affiliations and a gradual shift in social structure as coastal populations grew, changes which had occurred many years earlier in northern Florida.

For several hundred years between A.D. 1 and 400, the Crystal River site, a state archaeological park open to the public, was an important town-center, one that must have controlled trade along much of that coast. Shell platform mounds—one huge before a third of it was removed in the 1960s—and mounds and associated earthworks for the burial of villagers were constructed. The largest earthwork at the site is the one that harbored a rich assortment of late Deptford and early Weeden Island period artifacts, many of which were exotic items similar to artifacts utilized by Hopewellian cultures elsewhere in the Southeast.

The site's occupants were blessed by a favorable environment, being located on the Crystal River itself, near the Gulf, and adjacent to an expanse of hardwood forest. But the Crystal River villagers were not able to sustain their favored status and the site's importance waned, possibly to be replaced by first one and then another of the two town-centers dating to the Weeden Island period and located near the coast in Dixie County near Horseshoe Beach. Still later, after A.D. 1000, the locus of important town-centers seems to have shifted southward to Tampa Bay. Not a single late precolumbian town-center is known for the north peninsular coast.

The native cultures of the central Gulf coast region—Pasco, Hillsborough, Pinellas, Manatee, and Sarasota counties—are related to their northern neighbors, though there are important differences. A major rea-

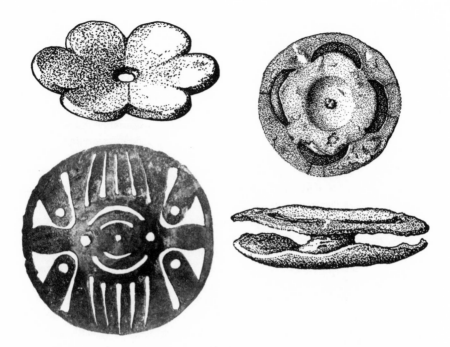

Decorative items from the Crystal River site, all at the same scale. *Upper left*, shell ornament, 2 1/2 inches across; *lower left*, one side of a copper ear spool; *right*, two views of a silver-covered copper ear spool. The spools are worn in holes in the ear lobes.

son for those differences is the presence of Tampa Bay, a large estuary that once provided copious amounts of fish and shellfish for native people living along its shores. The importance of the bay as a source of food for Indian societies should not be underestimated; the total length of its indented shoreline is nearly equal to the entire Gulf shoreline of the central coast. For the occupants of the region, Tampa Bay was a giant seafood market capable of supporting relatively denser native populations. More people meant more integrated sociopolitical systems. As a result the archaeological assemblages of this region after 500 B.C. exhibit less of the diversity found to the north.

Today Tampa Bay and the central Gulf coast look little like they did in the past. The extensive mangroves and salt marshes are gone and many interior wetlands have been drained. Worse, portions of the large and numerous shell middens that once dominated bayside and shoreline estuaries were carted off around the turn of the century to pave roads in Tampa, Bradenton, and other towns. Others were simply bulldozed to make room

◇ · ◇ · ◇ · ◇ · ◇ · ◇ · ◇ · ◇ · ◇

## The Famous Crystal River Site

During the first two decades of the twentieth century, Philadelphia-based archaeologist Clarence B. Moore mounted three expeditions to investigate the Crystal River site. What he found continues to draw the attention of archaeologists and was instrumental in the site becoming Florida's first state archaeological park and earning it considerable fame.

Within the largest sand mound and its surrounding earthen platform and embankment at Crystal River, Moore excavated an array of late Deptford and early Weeden Island period artifacts. The Indians who lived at Crystal River must have obtained these ceremonial and valued items through trade routes that ultimately connected with other societies in and well beyond Florida. Some trading may have been via canoes plying the inshore waters of the Gulf and leading up the Apalachicola River into the interior of the Southeast.

Comparisons with the much later Lake Jackson artifacts (chapter 5) help to point out the range, diversity, and complexity of native American crafts and beliefs. Included in the caches of Crystal River objects excavated by Moore were copper pan pipes; copper ear spools, some with silver on them (a natural occurrence in some copper deposits) and one with pearl insets; elongate plummets of copper, shell, and stone; a cut panther jaw and the worked teeth of bears and other carnivores, objects thought to be parts of masks; two-hole, stone bar gorgets; cut shell ornaments, including one in the shape of a flower with petals; and platform-shaped clay smoking pipes.

With these shell, stone, and copper items were a variety of ceremonial ceramic vessels: miniature pots; a four-lobed tetrapodal vessel; and a doughnut-shaped vessel with three spouts. Some incised, painted, and negative painted vessels from the earthwork are nearly unique to the site, being extremely rare in other mounds of the same time. Others—such as Deptford, Swift Creek, and St. Johns vessels—are more common throughout the region. The platform and embankment, the later parts of the earthwork, yielded a number of ceremonial containers like those found at northern Florida Weeden Island sites.

The elaborate Crystal River earthwork was utilized as a burial ground over at least several hundred years, perhaps as many as 400. Today the site is in public hands and will be protected and preserved forever, a monument to the Indians who once lived there.

◇ · ◇ · ◇ · ◇ · ◇ · ◇ · ◇ · ◇ · ◇

Stone plummets from the Crystal River site (the round one in the center has a diameter just over an inch and a half). Archaeologists still are not sure whether plummets were used as ornaments, net weights, weights for weaving, or for some other purpose.

for coastal developments. With them went important evidence of our Native American heritage. But some sites remain and with information excavated in the late nineteenth and early twentieth centuries, as well as during the federal relief programs in the 1930s, archaeologists continue to refine our knowledge of the central peninsula Gulf coast Indian cultures.

Archaeologists have given the name Manasota culture to the coastal dwellers of 500 B.C. to A.D. 750, a period contemporary with the Deptford and early Weeden Island cultures of northern Florida. As in the north peninsular Gulf coast region, Manasota sites are shell middens frequently clustered around the mouths and lower portions of rivers and streams draining into Tampa Bay or the Gulf. Some were large ridges, at times with high mounds with ramps or ridges leading to their tops. It seems likely that many of the sites were occupied over hundreds of years. Coastal bounty allowed the same locations to be used for many generations. Although only a small sample of such sites remains, one cannot help but notice that many of the central coast shell midden sites are more like the sites of southwest Florida than those of the north peninsular coast.

Not all Manasota sites are on the coast. Small settlements and special-use camps are found in the interior pine woods on higher ground near wetlands. Occasionally, in the best locations, larger villages are found, such as on the Myakkahatchee River. Even so, the main Manasota occupation was on the coast, where it was easiest to make a living.

Mounds were not used in the Manasota region until after A.D. 100; prior to that time the Indians of the region interred their dead in their shell middens or in burial grounds at villages. The earliest mounds, after A.D. 100, were not associated with charnel houses. But after A.D. 300, charnel house use is indicated. Weeden Island ceremonial vessels also were placed in mounds during that time. As on the north peninsular coast, these changes probably reflect the increased importance of lineage affiliation and the growth of regional communities and community identity.

The basic economic patterns of the central coast were well established by 500 B.C. and continued to be practiced by the Manasota people. Cultural changes that did occur in the region late in Manasota times, after A.D. 750, were not related to environmental changes but to social changes. With larger populations, people had to implement new social and political systems that would allow them to use the resources around them more effectively. Agriculture was not the answer; the soils around Tampa Bay and those away from the coast were not well suited to slash-and-burn farming.

Instead, more effective social and political systems were needed—in short, greater bureaucracy, more centralized leadership, and a social system that maximized the use of the wild resources of specific territories.

Changes began slowly and then increased in tempo. The interval between A.D. 750 and about 900 was probably a time of great change as new ideas, some borrowed from more northerly cultures and from southwest Florida, were put in place and adjusted so that they worked for the central coast region. By A.D. 900 a new culture had emerged. The Safety Harbor culture, while centered on Tampa Bay, ultimately extended from the Withlacoochee River in the north to Charlotte Harbor in the south.

As with the preceding cultures, most Safety Harbor sites—shell middens and shell and/or earth mounds—are on the coast. But a significant number of villages, camps, and mounds are in Polk, Hardee, and DeSoto counties and the inland portions of the coastal counties. The subsistence patterns of the Safety Harbor coastal people were like those of their predecessors: hunting, gathering wild plant foods, and fishing. A single squash seed from a mound in the Cove of the Withlacoochee in Citrus County corroborates sixteenth-century Spanish accounts describing agricultural fields and the cultivation of corn north of about Dade City, well north of Tampa Bay. Corn was seen by the Narváez expedition in the Indian town of Tocobaga at the north end of Old Tampa Bay, but corn is not mentioned in any accounts from the Hernando de Soto expedition describing the Safety Harbor people living on the east side of Tampa Bay. In general in precolumbian Florida, it appears that corn was not grown south of an east-west line drawn from the coast west of Dade City through Lake George on the St. Johns River to just north of Cape Canaveral.

The heartland of the Safety Harbor culture was around Tampa Bay in Pinellas, Hillsborough, Manatee, and northern Sarasota counties, south of the agricultural region. The people who built and occupied the town-centers around the bay—centers for small chiefdoms—were not farmers but subsisted primarily on fish and shellfish. For that reason larger chiefdoms did not develop; the prominence of one chiefdom vis-à-vis its neighbors probably rose and fell as a result of local warfare.

Each of these chiefdoms had a distinct territory, which included both land along the bay proper, roughly 15 miles of shoreline, and the area inland for some distance, perhaps 20 or more miles. In each chiefdom the chief and some of the populace lived at a modest capital town; other smaller settlements and camps were scattered along the shore and inland.

Each capital included houses for villagers and one or more mounds on which buildings—temples and chiefly residences—were erected. Other mounds and charnel houses were located nearby.

Over time, capitals were abandoned and new ones founded, leaving at least 15 such sites across the landscape, a few of which still exist. They are impressive testimony to Florida's Indians, and it is fortunate that some are in public ownership and are afforded protection. Other sites, not as lucky, have been totally obliterated by modern construction projects. But thanks to Clarence B. Moore, the same archaeologist who excavated Mt. Royal in east Florida, we have drawings and information for a few of the mound complex sites that have disappeared under greater Tampa.

The plan of the various Safety Harbor capitals is similar: a platform mound—the base for an important building—fronts a plaza that is surrounded by shell middens, refuse discarded by the villagers who lived in houses around the plaza. Mounds (usually one, sometimes more) used for burials also were built at each capital as well as at other settlements, both

◇ · ◇ · ◇ · ◇ · ◇ · ◇ · ◇ · ◇ · ◇ ·

## Chiefly Remains

A Spanish account penned in the 1560s describes the ritual cleaning of a Safety Harbor chief's mortal remains. Probably the source of the description is the Spaniards led by Pedro Menéndez de Avilés, governor of Spanish Florida, who sailed to the town of Tocobaga on Old Tampa Bay.

### Memorial of the Indians and Ceremonies of the Indians of Tocobaga

When a cacique [chief] from the leading ones dies, they break him into pieces and [macerate them] in some large jars and they [macerate them] two days until the flesh separates from the bones and they take the bones and they join one bone with another until they mount the man as he was and they place him in a house that they have as a temple while they fast four days. At the end of the four days they assemble all the people of the village and go out with him to the procession and they [inter the bones], making many reverences to him, and then they say that all those who go to the procession gain indulgences. (In John H. Hann, *Missions to the Calusa* [Gainesville: University Presses of Florida, 1991], p. 318)

◇ · ◇ · ◇ · ◇ · ◇ · ◇ · ◇ · ◇ · ◇ ·

on the coast and inland. Some burial mounds apparently were built far away from any settlement.

Each platform mound typically was 20 feet or less in height, its rectangular base 130 feet or less on a side; a ramp extended up the side toward the plaza. At least some mounds, perhaps all, were periodically rebuilt, increasing in size as new layers were added. As with Fort Walton platform mounds, the mound additions probably correlated with the rebuilding of structures on the mound.

Unlike in Fort Walton and other Mississippian platform mounds, chiefly individuals or members of their family were not buried in tombs dug down into the mounds. Instead they were interred in their lineage mound after their remains had been ritually cleaned. Family members may have been interred in the same mound after their remains had been stored and cleaned in a temple that served as a charnel house.

One member of the Hernando de Soto expedition described what a Safety Harbor capital looked like. I believe the town is Uzita, which was the Thomas site on the north side of the Little Manatee River in southern Hillsborough County. The site was destroyed in the twentieth century to make room for agricultural fields and a trailer park.

> The town was of seven or eight houses, built of timber, and covered with palm-leaves. The Chief's house stood near the beach, upon a very high mount made by hand for defence; at the other end of the town was a temple, on the top of which perched a wooden fowl with gilded eyes. (Edward G. Bourne, ed., and trans., *Narratives of the Career of Hernando de Soto in the Conquest of Florida* . . . [New York: A. S. Barnes and Co., 1866], 1:22–23)

The Safety Harbor culture in the Tampa Bay region does bear some resemblances to the Fort Walton culture in northwest Florida, such as in the use of platform mounds and chiefly political organization. But Safety Harbor was not a Mississippian culture. As noted, the Tampa Bay villagers were not farmers, and population densities, though larger than in some other localities along the central and northern Gulf coast, were much less than in the Fort Walton region. The relatively less dense populations and the resulting lack of available labor for community projects may be reflected in the practice of enlarging older Weeden Island burial mounds and turning them in Safety Harbor platform mounds, rather than building from scratch.

A Safety Harbor water bottle from Hillsborough County. Ten inches high, the bottle is decorated with hands, a Southeastern Ceremonial Complex motif.

Other traits shared with Fort Walton included some Southeastern Ceremonial Complex iconography. The Safety Harbor people must have borrowed from their northern neighbors, as did the Timucuan people to the north. Symbols related to Mississippian beliefs concerning warfare and adoration of chiefly ancestors are present in the Safety Harbor region in the form of designs incised on ceremonial ceramic vessels; but symbols surrounding agricultural fertility are not. To help support the concepts of chiefly lineages and territoriality, some ideas were borrowed; others, because they were not needed, were not.

As we would expect in a society organized as a chiefdom, lineage affiliation manifested in burial mounds and charnel houses seems to have been common in Safety Harbor culture. We have a firsthand description of charnel house use from 1539. In that year, soldiers from the Hernando de Soto expedition were scouting the countryside around Uzita when they encountered a strange apparition running at them. Fortunately for Juan Ortiz, the soldiers did not shoot first and ask questions later.

The soldiers learned that Ortiz had been left behind by his companions when he and other Spaniards had sailed into Tampa Bay 11 years earlier searching for the Narváez expedition. Ortiz had been captured by Indians and, in the intervening years, had lived with two different Safety Harbor chiefdoms on Tampa Bay. One chief had assigned him to guard the chiefly lineage's charnel house:

> When Ortiz got well, he was put to watching a temple, that the
> wolves, in the night-time, might not carry off the dead there. . . . One
> night they snatched away from him the body of a little child, son of a
> principal man; and, going after them, he threw a dart at the wolf that
> was escaping, which, feeling itself wounded, let go its hold, and went
> off to die. (Bourne, *Narratives,* p. 30)

At times charnel houses were built on mounds, and often two or even more were built one atop the other.

Are we certain that the descriptions cited above from the narratives of the de Soto expedition depict the Safety Harbor peoples? We are. Some people may wish to argue that de Soto landed in Charlotte Harbor or somewhere else in southwest Florida, but the overwhelming evidence all points toward Tampa Bay.

Both of the early sixteenth-century Spanish expeditions, those of Narváez and de Soto, traveled northward from Tampa Bay through the region of the Safety Harbor culture. Participants on both expeditions

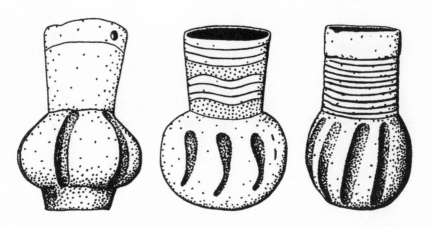

Three Safety Harbor gourd-effigy ceramic vessels. The left vessel is just under 6 inches tall. Archaeologist George Luer suggests that these and similar vessels were used in the brewing of medicines.

wrote accounts of their treks and today those narratives are available to be read and used in enhancing our understanding of Florida's Indians.

The Narváez and de Soto expedition accounts, among the earliest describing the native peoples of the United States, indicate that as many as 1,000 Spaniards were in Safety Harbor territory for two to five months. No wonder then that artifacts believed to be from those early encounters—glass and metal beads and iron hardware—are still being found today; the expeditions gave away and lost a large number of objects. Such artifacts, excavated from a number of Safety Harbor sites, are incontrovertible evidence that the Safety Harbor people were living in the region in the sixteenth century when Spanish colonizing, military, and diplomatic expeditions came to Tampa Bay.

Many metal decorative items, such as silver discs, also have been found. Their source is probably Spanish ships wrecked on the shallow Gulf coast, their cargoes later salvaged by the Indians. Fleets and individual ships laden with booty from the Americas sailed from Veracruz in Mexico and then navigated the coasts of Florida before sailing across the Atlantic. Not all made the journey successfully, and those that came to grief provided a source of exotic goods to the Safety Harbor Indians. Silver and even gold artifacts that the Spaniards had wrested from the Indians of South and Central America and Mexico were salvaged, some to be reworked by native people in Florida.

Glass, metal, and ceramic artifacts preserved in sites are only the tip of the salvage iceberg. Cloth, clothing, wooden objects, and many other items were salvaged, but they have not been preserved. Members of the first Spanish expedition to land on the Gulf coast, that of Narváez, were amazed at the salvaged goods they saw and at the uses to which items had been put. In a Safety Harbor village at the north end of Old Tampa Bay, probably the town of Tocobaga, the Spaniards were shown wooden boxes salvaged from ships; human remains were stored in the boxes, carefully wrapped in painted deer hides. They also saw linen, cloth, feather headdresses, and small amounts of gold.

◇  ·  ◇  ·  ◇  ·  ◇  ·  ◇  ·  ◇  ·  ◇  ·  ◇  ·  ◇  ·

### Safety Harbor Charnel Houses

In 1934 archaeologist D. L. Reichard excavated a mound near Parrish, Florida, inland near the Little Manatee River in Manatee County. The flat-topped mound, 65 feet in diameter and 6 feet high, had been built atop a Safety Harbor charnel house. Before mound construction commenced, this first building was dismantled and its wooden parts, as well as the human remains stored in it, were burned in a large pit. The pit was then buried under the mound.

Then a second wooden charnel house was erected. It was rectangular to trapezoidal, 25 feet on a side with wall posts 5 to 10 inches in diameter placed about 6 inches apart.

One corner was reinforced with a second row of posts that extended 6 feet along one wall and 7 feet along the other. Inside, in that corner of the house, human remains were cremated and then buried under the floor. More cremated remains were buried outside the building, including two people interred in small pits lined and covered with logs. Chert points and tools and shell cups were found along with an owl effigy bottle and European artifacts.

How did the Safety Harbor people deal with the horrible increase in deaths resulting from the epidemics fueled by diseases brought to their land by the Europeans? Perhaps cremation of bodies became a part of the burial ritual.

Eventually the entire charnel house was burned to the ground and the mound abandoned. The charred roof supports and wall posts gradually were covered by debris, lying undisturbed until their discovery centuries later. Recent attempts to find this mound have failed. Evidently it has been lost to twentieth-century development.

◇  ·  ◇  ·  ◇  ·  ◇  ·  ◇  ·  ◇  ·  ◇  ·  ◇  ·  ◇  ·

The relatively sudden appearance of such goods, not to mention the shipwrecked Europeans salvaged with the cargoes, must have been extraordinary events. New wealth and strange foreigners could only have led to more competition between Safety Harbor groups seeking to garner wealth and status. The sixteenth century brought a new world to the Florida Indians.

It is ironic that although the invading expeditions of Narváez and de Soto—and even the excursions to Tampa Bay in the mid-1560s by Spaniards led by Pedro Menéndez de Avilés, founder of St. Augustine—provide important firsthand accounts of Safety Harbor lifeways, those same Spanish entradas had severe negative impacts on native life. Military actions, the introduction of European diseases, and the enslavement of native people as consorts and bearers resulted in deaths and the political and demographic collapse of chiefdoms.

At the time de Soto's army camped in the Safety Harbor town of Uzita on the Little Manatee River, there were at least three chiefdoms around the bay: Uzita, territory of which extended from the Little Manatee River south and west to Sarasota Bay; Mocoso, on the east side of Hillsborough Bay, encompassing the Alafia and, perhaps, the Hillsborough rivers; and Tocobaga, on Old Tampa Bay. Within the territories of each of these chiefdoms are several village-mound archaeological sites, former chiefly capitals. In at least one capital in each locality, artifacts brought by Spaniards or salvaged from Spanish ships have been found.

A fourth chiefdom might also have been on the bay at the time of de Soto. Capeloey possibly was on the upper portion of the bay and its territory might have included the Hillsborough River; the people of Capeloey may be the same people later referred to as the Pohoy.

The impact of the Spanish presence on the Safety Harbor chiefdoms was immediate. Twenty-five years after de Soto, the Uzita and Mocoso chiefdoms no longer existed. Remnant groups of those people may have joined other groups. The most powerful chiefdom on the bay in the 1560s was led by chief Tocobaga. But the people of Tocobaga also would suffer at the hands of the Spaniards, and the Pohoy Indians would assume the mantle of power, only to be attacked by Spaniards in 1612 in retribution for Pohoy raids on Spanish missions.

Eighty years after the first European sailed into Tampa Bay, the Safety Harbor people had effectively been decimated and their chiefdoms had been destroyed. The names Uzita and Mocoso never appear again in documents after the invasion of the de Soto expedition. Some people, remnants of those and other populations, continued to live on the bay, sometimes under new names given them by the Spaniards. The Alafaia (Alafia) Indians are probably one such group. By 1679 the remnant Pohoy still living on the bay had been militarily coopted by a Calusa chief from southwest Florida who had extended his power all the way to Tampa Bay, filling the power vacuum left with the demise of the Safety Harbor chiefs.

Others of the Tampa Bay Indians fled northward. In the early eighteenth century, a few Tocobaga and Pohoy people were living in refugee villages around St. Augustine. About the same time, 1718, a village of refugee Tocobaga living at the mouth of the Wacissa River in former Apalachee Indian territory was attacked by a group of their old neighbors, the Pohoy. Perhaps the Pohoy were settling old scores.

The new world that began for the Safety Harbor Indians in the sixteenth century proved to be their undoing. Could the Indians who watched de Soto's troops unload supplies and move into their village in late spring of 1539 ever have thought that by two centuries later, their way of life would have been totally destroyed? Could anyone have foreseen that in another two centuries, archaeological remains of the Safety Harbor people whose ancestors had lived around Tampa Bay for more than 4,000 years would be road fill?

# 7 Belle Glade, Glades, and Caloosahatchee Cultures

If the precolumbian Gulf coast of Florida can be described as soggy, then the southern third of the state can only be said to have been positively wet. Today south Florida, the scene of a century of massive drainage projects, is relatively dry compared to what it once was. One hundred and fifty years ago, anyone who tried to get from Miami to Fort Myers on the Tamiami Trail would have needed water wings.

At that time the interior of southern Florida was largely a giant wetland; a massive sheet of water flowed slowly southward down the peninsula, threading its way through sawgrass and swamp. The largest expanse of open water was Lake Okeechobee, its size was nearly twice what it is at present. Before its southerly end was drained in the late nineteenth century, it simply trailed off into the Everglades. South Florida was the original water world.

Dry land—whether adjacent to Gulf or Atlantic shore, on an Everglades hammock, or along the banks of the Kissimmee and Caloosahatchee rivers—was prime real estate, attracting precolumbian Indians. That wet environment fostered the development of three regional cultures. In the Lake Okeechobee Basin with its considerable expanses of freshwater wetlands was the distinctive Belle Glade culture, which flourished after 1000 B.C. On the other side of the state, east of Lake Okeechobee and south and east to the Atlantic coast and into the Florida Keys, was the Glades culture. What today is the Dade County Gold Coast was once the home of the Tequesta Indians, whose Glades ancestors plied the waters of Biscayne Bay and the Everglades proper, canoeing out from their main village at the mouth of the Miami River. Other native groups, many of whose names we do not even know, also were associated with the Glades culture.

The shallow inshore waters of the southwest coast—among the most productive in Florida for net fishing and whelk collecting—were home to a third culture, the Caloosahatchee, whose origins can be traced back to the end of the Late Archaic cultures of the region prior to 500 B.C. In the colonial period, southwest Florida was the land of the Calusa Indians, who greeted Juan Ponce de León when he landed there in 1513 and sent him packing when he returned in 1521.

The people of these three cultures, Belle Glade, Glades, and Caloosa-hatchee, all lived by hunting, fishing, and foraging for wild foods, although there is evidence suggesting that at least for a time, the villagers around Lake Okeechobee grew corn. Throughout their histories, the people of these cultures exchanged ideas and traded with one another as well as with cultures farther north. They were well aware of their social and natural surroundings. Some archaeologists are incredulous that they were not in contact with Caribbean Indians as well, but as yet evidence for such pre-historic connections has not been found.

The south Florida cultures differed from one another in important ways, in large part because of their particular settings in south Florida: south-west coast versus Okeechobee region versus Everglades, Atlantic coast, and Keys. Population densities and the nature of sociopolitical and settlement systems diverged. South Florida well illustrates the cultural ingenuity of Florida's Indians.

## Belle Glade Culture

If you were to ask me which precolumbian Florida Indian culture I find most interesting, I would first try to avoid answering. But if pressed, I would have to admit it is Belle Glade. The reason is simple. In 1966 I was an undergraduate mathematics major who enrolled in an introductory an-thropology course as one of my electives. Soon I learned about something called archaeological field school: sign up and spend a summer term learn-ing about archaeology and the south Florida Indians by excavating at Fort Center, a Belle Glade site on the west side of Lake Okeechobee. On a sunny late April day, I opened the car door in Glades County and stepped into the past. After only a few days of looking at maps and photographs, wandering around the countryside, and rising at 5:30 A.M. to work in the field, I was hooked on archaeology and on the remarkable Belle Glade culture. The rest, as they say, is history.

Fort Center, named for a Second Seminole War fort built on the site, stretches for nearly a mile along the banks of Fisheating Creek. It is the most intensively studied Belle Glade site, thanks to the late William H. Sears, archaeologist at Florida Atlantic University, who directed research there for six years. Fort Center is one of nearly two dozen large earthwork sites, all of which are on or near the old shoreline of Lake Okeechobee. Similar sites are found along the Caloosahatchee and Kissimmee rivers, and smaller midden sites, some of which may have been single family households, are scattered across the Okeechobee Basin landscape, just north of the Everglades.

The Belle Glade region takes in all or inland portions of Glades, Hendry, Palm Beach, and Martin counties around the lake. To the north, sites extend up through Okeechobee and Highlands counties into Osceola and Polk. Many of the sites in this extended region, both large and small, are visible on aerial photographs taken in the 1940s. Since that time, however, many sites have been flattened or bulldozed by drainage projects and the expansion of pasture. Federal projects to channelize the Kissimmee River cut through some sites and buried others under dredged spoil.

The earthworks at Fort Center are typical of those found in the basin: mounds, ponds, borrows, circular ditches, and linear embankments. Circular embankments and peculiar, geometric-shaped earthworks are known from other sites, and middens—often containing rich dark organic deposits—were once common wherever there was dry land. Even subtle differences in elevation affect drainage in this region. Consequently differences in vegetation often are clues to site locations, as are wallows where cows congregate and dig shallow depressions in which to lie and cool off.

Can cows find archaeological sites? Probably not, but they are smart enough to seek relief from the sun by lying in the shade of palm trees, which grow in higher, drier areas. Belle Glade people once sought these same locations, where their refuse and activities resulted in the accumulation of middens, adding to the elevation. Even when scrub vegetation was plowed under to plant pasture, these higher hammocks survived—damaged but not totally destroyed—and became good habitat for palm trees and cows. As a junior archaeologist, I quickly learned to look out across

An aerial photograph of Tony's Mound. The small white dots on the right are cows.

Tony's Mound. The scale is in meters, a meter being slightly more than 3 feet.

60 meters

hundreds of acres of pasture, spot the palms and cows, and find another midden.

These small, presumably household middens remain largely unstudied. It is the large sites that have drawn the attention of archaeologists since the 1930s, sites like Fort Center and Ortona (both in Glades County), Big Mound City and Belle Glade (Palm Beach County), and Tony's Mound (Hendry County). The size of these unique sites is staggering. I once visited Big Mound City on the east side of the lake. Even armed with a map and an aerial photograph, it still took me several mosquito-filled hours to correlate what was on the ground with my maps. The problem was that my mind refused to believe that what was so small on a photograph was in reality so large.

Big Mound City, as well as Tony's Mound and certain other earthwork sites, have been labeled "Big Circle" sites, a reference to the semicircular or horseshoe-shaped sand embankments at each. Extending out from every one of these annular earthworks, which average about 500 feet across at their openings, are five to ten linear embankments, each usually with a small round or oval mound on its end. Within the opening of every Big Circle earthwork is a large mound composed of midden. Big Circle sites also feature other mounds and earthworks like those at Fort Center.

Another type of earthwork in the Belle Glade region, as well as in the Caloosahatchee region to the west, is canals, such as those at Ortona. Canals, some of them several miles long, were dug to facilitate canoe travel between villages and rivers. Huge earthen embankments and miles-long canals are not the only extraordinary human-made Belle Glade earthworks. Aerial photographs of the Okeechobee Basin reveal several sites with circular ditches 375 to 440 yards across. And there are still more types of earthworks. Fort Center and several other sites feature small, human-made ponds.

Why were these earthen structures, ditches, and ponds built? When were they built? What were they used for? Questions to which I wanted instant explanations 30 years ago gradually have been answered, in large part by the excavations carried out at Fort Center. But those same investigations have raised other queries, puzzles we still cannot satisfactorily solve. Using what was learned from William Sears's Fort Center project as a guide, let us look at the Belle Glade culture and its curious sites.

Fort Center was chosen for study because it contains most of the array of earthwork constructions present in the basin; missing are only canals

Plate 1. Unique in Florida, this small ceramic object (about 4½ inches high) has zones of red painting. It was excavated from Franklin County and dates to the late Deptford–early Swift Creek period, about A.D. 1–100. It may have been a small ceremonial water drum used with membranes over both openings.

Plate 2. A zoned rocker-stamped ceramic vessel from Bay County has a design made by walking a small tool on the surface of the clay and then enclosing the motif in zones (or vice versa). Associated with the Santa Rosa–Swift Creek Culture, A.D. 100–300, the 9-inch-high vessel has decoration similar to that found on contemporary Hopewell culture ceramics in the Ohio River Valley.

Plate 3. Also from Bay County, this early Weeden Island (A.D. 300 to 750) effigy of a great horned owl is about 8½ inches high.

Plate 4. This painted Weeden Island urn from the Buck Mound in Walton County is 15 inches high. Radiocarbon dates for the mound range from A.D. 500 to 800.

Plate 5. An early Weeden Island bird-effigy from Bay County, 9 inches high, dates from A.D. 300 to 750.

Plate 6. It is not certain how this 11¼-inch-high early Weeden Island ceramic container from Bay County was used. Perhaps it is was part of an apparatus used to brew ceremonial teas.

Plate 7. An early Weeden Island effigy from Franklin County, is 8 inches high.

Plate 8. An incised bowl 6 inches in diameter from Walton County is from a Weeden Island mound and exhibits a Weeden Island–like motif, though the design also resembles some from the Fort Walton culture.

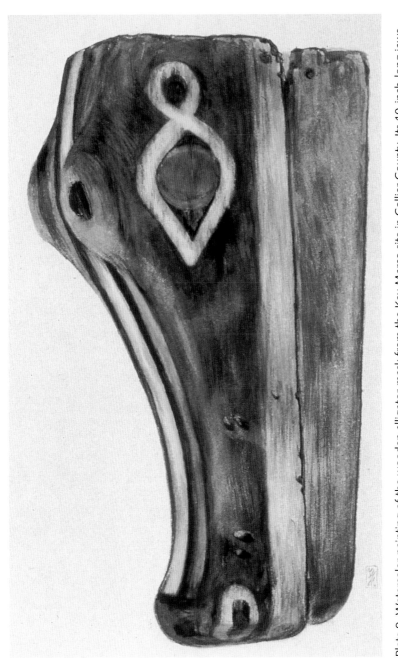

Plate 9. Watercolor painting of the wooden alligator mask from the Key Marco site in Collier County. Its 10-inch-long jaws articulate. The painting is by Wells Sawyer, who accompanied the expedition led by Frank Hamilton Cushing that excavated the site in 1895–96.

Plate 10. Paintings of two of the painted wooden masks from the Key Marco site, both by Wells Sawyer. Each is about 8 inches high. When removed from the muck where they had been preserved for hundreds of years, these and other wooden masks warped and shrank and some fell to pieces.

Plate 11. Paintings of two wooden plaques or amulets from the Key Marco site by Wells Sawyer. Both fell apart after excavation, though fragments of one still exist. In Cushing's catalogue at the Smithsonian Institution's National Anthropological Archives, the one on the left is described as "in the form of a conventional spoonbill duck. Body incised with spirited figure of a dolphin." The one on the right exhibits the same complex spider motif found on colonial period metal objects in south Florida. No sizes were recorded, though Cushing's catalogue infers they were several inches long.

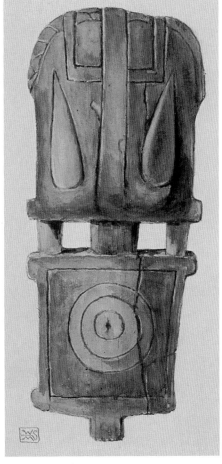

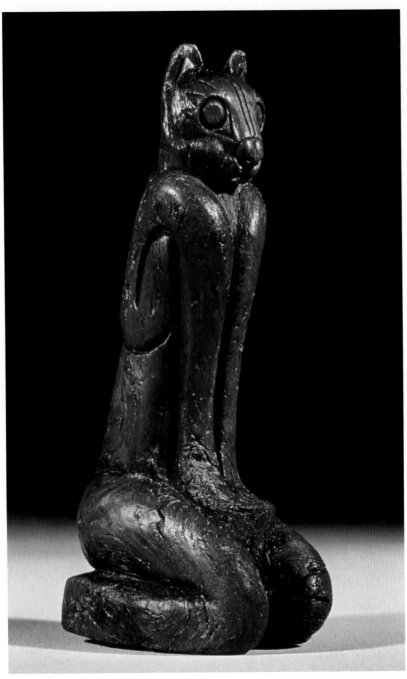

Plate 12. Perhaps the most famous single precolumbian object from Florida, this exquisite wooden carving of a kneeling panther also came from the Key Marco site. The 6-inch figurine may represent a person costumed as a panther.

Plate 13. Gold and silver ornaments from Glades County, made by Florida Indians from metal salvaged from Spanish shipwrecks. The rectangular gold ornament is 3½ inches long.

Plate 14. A buckskin shirt, beaded bandolier bag, 10-foot strand of faceted glass beads, fingerwoven beaded garter, Scotch-style beaded cap, and other accoutrements worn by a Seminole man in 1857. The two small leather pouches and the small, woven basket (with lid) were carried in the bandolier bag, along with the leather thong–wrapped, whittled stick. The cap was probably obtained through trade and was not a common item of Seminole apparel.

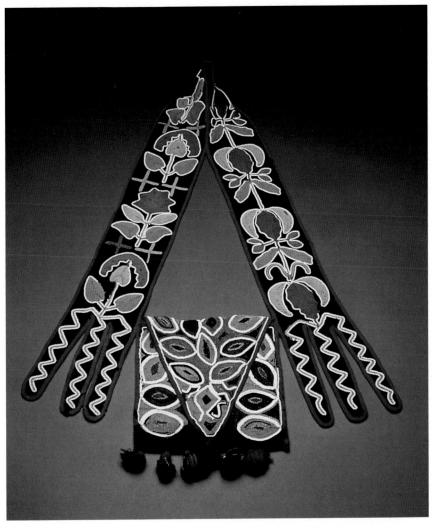

Plate 15. A Seminole beaded bandolier bag, probably dating from the 1830s.

Plate 16. Front and back views of a Seminole man's cloth long shirt with beaded, fingerwoven wrist garters. The shirt, trimmed with ruffles and strips of cloth similar to appliqué, is thought to be from the 1830s or 1840s.

and the horseshoe embankments. What was learned there could be used to interpret other Belle Glade sites.

We now know that the various Fort Center earthworks were built over at least 2,000 years. Within the basin the first Belle Glade settlements were occupied between 1000 and 500 B.C. Villagers made their living netting fish from the waters of Lake Okeechobee and collecting animals from the surrounding wetlands, especially turtles, snakes, and alligators. Some turtle shells were found with perforations, evidence that the turtles were tethered, to be eaten as needed. Fort Center villagers also hunted and caught land animals, though their main source of meat was the basin's wetlands. Strangely, few water birds were eaten.

Living at the site during its early period of occupation—prior to A.D. 200—were close to 100 people, who lived on the higher banks of Fisheating Creek or nearby on small mounds built to keep their homes above flood waters. The creek, a good-sized meandering stream, not only provided food; it also was a canoe highway leading to Lake Okeechobee and its resources, several miles away.

A variety of stone, bone, and shell artifacts were found in the middens. Shark teeth, hafted either singly or in groups by perforating, notching, or thinning the bases, were used for cutting, carving, and sawing wood. Weaving shuttles, points, and gigs used for spearing fish, all of bone, were common, as were bone points or bits from bow drills, friction devices used to start fires.

Probably at the time the site was first occupied, villagers began constructing the first earthworks, a series of three overlapping circular ditches. The last one to be built, the largest, was 375 yards in diameter and averaged 28 feet in width at the top, with walls that sloped down to a flat bottom 6 feet below the ground surface. A radiocarbon date from charcoal discarded in the bottom of the ditch indicated that it had been built by 450 B.C.

While excavating portions of this ditch in 1966, we discovered that it had been built overlapping a slightly smaller, even earlier circular ditch. Subsequent examination of aerial photographs revealed still a third ditch, overlapped by the other two. The evidence, though unexpected, is overwhelming: before 500 B.C., perhaps several hundred years before, Belle Glade people were engaged in substantial earth-moving projects.

One explanation for the ditches, offered by William Sears, is that they were a way to drain water for fields in which corn was grown. Corn pollen was identified from soil samples collected from soil in the bottom of the latest ditch as well as from other places at the site. Sears theorized that because corn will not grow in wet places, people dug the ditches to cut through the underlying soil hardpan, allowing rainwater to drain better and keeping the central portion of the ditch and the area immediately around it dry.

Excavations indicated that water often accumulated in the ditch and that a mucky layer of organic material had collected there, probably including small fish and amphibians and their eggs. Sears suggested that periodically, this fertile muck could have been cleaned out and spread on the field, providing a "protoplasmic" fertilizer.

Sears also argued that the Okeechobee Basin resembles the lowlands of Mexico in terms of vegetation, rainfall patterns, growing season, and day length, making that area a possible location from which corn and the practice of drained-field cultivation were introduced across the Caribbean or around the Gulf of Mexico coast into southern Florida. If true, the Belle Glade corn complex would be one of the earliest, if not the earliest, of the precolumbian eastern United States.

But not everyone accepts that corn was grown in interior south Florida by 500 B.C. Some archaeologists argue that pollen can be washed down through the porous ground and can contaminate soil samples. Following Sears's excavations, soil cores taken from the ditch showed that at least in one place, one ditch was not dug deep enough to cut through the underlying hardpan layer. Analysis of the soils at the site also indicated low fertility, high aluminum, and high acidity, all factors that would have made Fort Center's soils poor for growing corn. In addition, Spanish documents make it certain that by the colonial period, corn was not being grown by any of the Indians living in south Florida. If corn was once grown there, it had ceased to be cultivated in later times.

The Fort Center circular ditches are not the only ones in the basin. A fourth ditch 420 yards in diameter lies several miles south of Fort Center, and another is southwest on the Caloosahatchee River. Others remain to be discovered. Questions such as these regarding corn agriculture and the circular ditches are just one reason I find the Belle Glade culture so intriguing.

Another reason also was prompted by Sears's excavations at Fort Center. From about A.D. 200 to about 600 to 800, a time when Sears believes the ditched fields were still being used, Belle Glade villagers built an extraordinary charnel center at the site. They began by digging an artificial pond 120 feet across and 5 feet deep. A portion of the removed fill was used

## A Sign from the Past

Truth is often stranger than fiction. In 1926 a hunter walking through the Fort Center site saw a headless wooden carving of an eagle sticking up out of a small pond beside a mound. He retrieved the carving, which proved to be a 5-foot tall post with a pointed base and a 27-inch eagle on top. The carving, made from dense pine, was exhibited for several years in front of a general store in Bartow, Florida, where it was seen by the director of the Florida State Museum.

In 1932, the eagle was transferred to the museum in Gainesville, where a head was sculpted and attached. Over the next four decades, with its new head, the carving was exhibited throughout the United States and even in England. To William Sears, who was an archaeologist at the museum from the 1950s to early 1960s, the eagle was a sign: excavate the pond! Using pumps and hoses he did just that, discovering one of the oldest collections of precolumbian wooden art in the United States.

But the story gets better. One of the objects found by Sears in the pond muck was a carved eagle head. No, it wasn't the one from the museum's eagle, but it must have been a twin to that one. When the old artificial head was removed, the new Fort Center head fit nicely. A cast was made and the eagle received its new head, one more delicate and gracile than the old.

About 1980, Sears sent all of the excavated Fort Center collections to the newly renamed Florida Museum of Natural History, reuniting the eagle with the other carvings. It was immediately obvious that the eagle, recovered in the 1920s, was in much better shape than the carvings excavated four decades later. The surfaces of the latter were eroded and many details had been lost. The eagle, on the other hand, still exhibited some of the shark tooth–tool carving scars made more than a millennium and a half earlier.

Why was this? Blame it on cows. Between 1926 and the time of Sears's investigations, cattle were pastured in and around the Fort Center site. The pond, with a shady tree at one end, was a convenient wading pool for cows to cool off in. It also served as a bovine bathroom. Over the years hooves and acidity severely eroded the wooden carvings, doing more damage than had 15 centuries in muck.

◇ · ◇ · ◇ · ◇ · ◇ · ◇ · ◇ · ◇ · ◇ ·

to build a low platform mound beside the pond; then a charnel house was erected on the mound.

Within the pond, which soon collected water, a D-shaped wooden platform was constructed out of timbers, including inverted tree stumps placed underneath for support. Posts, the upper portions of which were carved in the shape of animals, helped to suspend the platform above the water level in the pond. The bottoms of the carved posts were pushed down and anchored in the pond bottom. Other carvings adorned the sides of the platform, on which bundles of human bones were laid after the bodies of the deceased had first been processed in the charnel house. At some point, loaded with the remains of 150 or so individuals, the platform was partially burned, and it then collapsed into the pond.

Bundles of human remains were salvaged from the pond and placed on a layer of clean sand deposited on the floor of the charnel house, after the building itself was removed. Several alternating layers of remains and clean sand were laid down before a final mound cap was added, resulting in a mound 14 feet high.

The wooden platform elements and carvings preserved in the muck in the bottom of the pond represent an incredible array of wildlife: life-size cats, a bear, foxes, and larger-than-life birds, including two eagles and wading birds. Smaller carvings with tenon bases were positioned along the edges of the platform on the tops of mortised posts. Still other wooden carvings—such as an exquisitely fashioned running otter with a fish in its mouth—and objects, tools, and a set of carved, wooden deer antlers also were preserved. Most likely, the animals depicted held the same symbolic importance in the Belle Glade belief system as the animals portrayed on Weeden Island effigy ceramic vessels in northern Florida.

At the opposite side of the pond from this mound was a dense midden that Sears believes was deposited in and around a building housing the people who performed the charnel activities. Even after the collapse of the platform and the building of the burial mound, people continued to live there.

I believe that the building could have been a men's lodge, where Belle Glade males lounged, chipped tools, smoked their pipes, and carved the wooden platform supports. They also performed the rituals and duties associated with caring for the dead. The midden associated with their lodge contained fired clay platform pipes; a cache of chert nodules (raw material used to chip stone tools); and shell, shark-tooth, and stone wood-carving

Drawing of the carved wooden eagle from the Fort Center site
pond with its new head

tools. Overall, the artifact assemblage from this midden was unlike that found anywhere else at the site.

After the halt of charnel activities, Fort Center continued to be home to villagers who lived adjacent to the creek. The importance of the site as a center for communal activities seems to have drawn to a close; perhaps that importance was assumed by another site in the basin.

Later, after A.D. 1200–1400 and extending into the colonial period, new earthwork construction began. Sears suggests that the circular, ditched fields, long abandoned, were replaced by linear, raised earthen embankments. These linear embankments, like those at the Big Circle sites, measure 180 to more than 580 feet in length and some have circular house mounds built on one end. It is this type of linear embankment that is present at many of the other mound complex sites in the Okeechobee region, such as Big Mound City and Tony's Mound.

Did these embankments function as raised fields, a way to keep corn plants above their wet surroundings and maximize fertility by piling organic material on low earthworks? It is uncertain. Corn agriculture in the Okeechobee Basin remains a controversy that will only be laid to rest with more field research.

Villagers were still living at Fort Center in the sixteenth and seventeenth centuries, when the site again seems to have had a reasonably large population and perhaps functioned as a center. Village chiefs might well have lived atop the older burial mound, burying their dead in the top of the mound. Individuals interred in the uppermost portion of the mound were accompanied by glass and metal beads and other objects salvaged by the Florida Indians from wrecked Spanish ships and brought to the site. Some of the metal was reworked by the Indians and fashioned into small metal plaques inscribed with various motifs, new versions of older, wooden plaques found elsewhere in south Florida.

Located in the interior, away from the coasts and the sites of shipwrecks the Belle Glade people were in a less advantageous location to compete with their neighbors to the east, south, and west. They also were not politically organized into a single political unit. Instead, the Belle Glade population was divided among separate, widely scattered earthwork-centers and outlying homesteads. It would be the Calusa Indians of the southwest coast who took the lead in expanding political influence through diplomacy and militarism to gain access to the new wealth washing up on Florida's shores.

## Glades Culture

After 500 B.C. and into the colonial period, the Belle Glade and Caloosahatchee cultures, the latter especially, occupied the most productive environmental zones in southern Florida. To their east and south, the natural
environments of the Glades culture were relatively less productive, although the Glades culture enjoyed the largest geographical extent.

The Glades culture region included a variety of wetlands: the Everglades, the large sawgrass marsh in Henry, Palm Beach, Broward, Dade,
and Monroe counties; the Big Cypress Swamp west of the Everglades in
Collier County; the extensive saltwater marshes and mangrove forests that
once characterized the coast but today have been almost totally destroyed
in Broward and Dade counties; and the shallow waters and saltwater mangroves and marshes of the Keys and mainland Monroe County.

Within this vast area, Glades sites were once clustered on the coasts,
especially on estuaries and where fresh water could be obtained, and along
the higher inland ridge that parallels the coast in southeast Florida. Sites
also dotted the high ground in the Big Cypress Swamp and in the Everglades, at times looking like islands in the sea of grass. Today only a small
sample of sites remains. Even sites recorded in the 1950s have been lost to
development. It is hard to imagine that early in the twentieth century, what
is now a row of glitzy hotels, apartments, and shops on Biscayne Bay was
shell middens.

The largest shell middens are along the coast, especially in the Ten
Thousand Island and Turner River regions on the productive southwest
coast south of the Caloosahatchee culture. Some village sites in this western coastal portion of the Glades region feature shellworks, including
embankments, mounds, and ramps. But good-sized shell middens also
were present on the Atlantic coast. They, too, must represent villages, as do
some of the Keys middens. Other, smaller coastal shell middens probably
were camps for fishing and oyster gathering. Still other special-use camps
are inland.

Not all Glades sites are shell middens. Some settlements in inland locales contain black earth middens, a reflection of high organic content
resulting from discarded refuse. Many of the intensely occupied small
sites—reused camps—in the Everglades are smaller versions of the rich
middens.

This picture of Glades settlements suggests that the people lived at central villages, some rather small, and traveled back and forth to camps to
hunt, fish, or for other purposes. Some movements may have been on a

seasonal basis, in addition to the much more frequent—almost daily—foraging and hunting trips. Compared to northern Florida or even to the Caloosahatchee region, the bulk of the Glades population was more scattered, a result of the hunting-gathering-fishing way of life and the nature of their environment, which did not support numerically large or dense populations. Basically the Glades people lived off fish and sharks, shellfish, reptiles (including sea turtles), and the products of a variety of wild plants, such as mastic, coco plum, cabbage palm, saw palmetto, sea grape, hog plum, acorns, and red mangrove sprouts.

Several villages or communities may have shared an identity, like the Tocobaga Indians living in the colonial period around the mouth of the Miami River, who recognized the chief of their main village as their leader. Other small chiefdomlike political units may also have existed elsewhere on the coasts. These all may have been attempts to copy the complex political system of the Caloosahatchee culture and the Calusa Indians, described later.

One site, perhaps as well known as the Crystal River site, deserves special mention. Key Marco on Marco Island in Collier County was excavated by archaeologist Frank Hamilton Cushing in 1896. On the northern end of the island just south of the southern boundary of the Caloosahatchee culture, Key Marco is another example of a site with organic materials preserved in wet deposits. Like Windover Pond and the charnel pond at Fort Center, Key Marco provides clues to the lifeways of Florida Indians that we cannot interpret from pieces of pottery or shell tools alone. As exceptional as the collection of artifacts from the site is, it probably only mirrors what was common in every Glades village in south Florida. Such wooden and fiber artifacts and remarkable art objects once would have been commonplace at all south Florida villages. Today, because they were fortuitously preserved in coastal muck deposits, they are an exceptional archaeological treasure.

The variety of wooden bowls, mortars and pestles, pounding tools (some look like dumbbells), boxes, trays, hafts or handles for adzes, knives, and other cutting tools is staggering. Some recovered tool handles still have the shell, bone, or shark teeth bits or working edges attached. And the handles are not just handles; several examples have been intricately carved, as have some of the long bone pins. The beauty of these everyday items is breathtaking. Also preserved in the Key Marco muck were a toy catamaran canoe, a canoe paddle, and throwing-stick handles and darts. The latter still were being used in south Florida thousands of years after we can first

This woodpecker, painted in black, white, and blue on a wooden board, perhaps a section of a box, is one of the many famous pieces of precolumbian
Indian art from the Key Marco site. Wells Sawyer, a member of the field team,
painted the 16-inch-long object shortly after it was excavated. A ghost image
of another animal—perhaps more than one—can be seen just below the bird's
claws. The original artist may not have completed the painting.

document their presence among the Archaic people. Most of the wood used to make the wooden tools and objects is cypress, buttonwood, or gumbo limbo.

Besides the decorated tool handles and bone pins, Cushing uncovered a number of other ornamented items—carved and sometimes painted wooden objects that further attest to the skills of the Glades people. Among the most famous items are the wooden masks, some with shell-inset eyes and others painted, used in ceremonies. There also are animal effigy masks, including a wolf head and an alligator. Both were composite masks with movable parts.

As spectacular as the masks are wooden plaques or "standards," several of which were just over 20 inches long. One, a rectangular, flat plank, was adorned with a painting of a woodpecker. Others were carved in relief in two sections with a tenon on one end. They appear to depict complex spider motifs. Another is carved with a dolphin. Two dolphins, tail to nose, were carved on a small piece of turtle shell.

Also among the Key Marco items are two carvings that are as magnificent as any examples of precolumbian Indian art from anywhere in the Americas: a painted deer head and a kneeling panther. The deer's ears are fitted with pegs to allow them to fit into the head. The panther appears to be a person in a costume, perhaps a figure from myth or ceremony.

The importance of fishing to the Glades people is reflected in the preserved sections of fiber netting, some with net floats and shell or stone weights still attached. Gourds and gourdlike small squashes functioned as net floats as well as containers. These plants were not cultivated but grew wild around native settlements, like those found at the St. Johns culture Hontoon Island site and at Windover Pond. Other items related to fishing included rectangular and square gauges made from bone and shell and used in weaving nets.

The Key Marco collection is unprecedented and provides a privileged view of what life was like for the precolumbian Florida Indians. Somewhere out there may be another Key Marco that will tell us even more. But in reality every site tells us something. What better reason to preserve the dwindling number of archaeological sites for future generations?

## Caloosahatchee Culture

If you, like me, find the Belle Glade culture with its remarkable mounds and embankments intriguing, you are certain to find the Caloosahatchee culture and its colonial period manifestation, the Calusa Indians, just as

Fifteen of the wooden masks from the Key Marco site. The human head in the lower right corner provides scale.

## The Political Realm of the Calusa Indians

Shipwrecked in south Florida about 1545 and rescued two decades later, the Spaniard Escalante de Fontaneda wrote this description of what he had learned:

> Running from south to north between Habana [Havana, Cuba] and Florida, the distance to the Tortugas [Dry Tortugas west of Key West] and the Martires [the Florida Keys] is forty leagues; twenty leagues to the Martires, and thence [an]other twenty to Florida—to the territory of Carlos, a province of Indians, which in their language signifies a fierce people, they are so-called for being brave and skillful, as in truth they are. They are masters of a large district of country, as far as a town they call Guacata, on the Lake of Mayaimi, which is called Mayaimi because it is very large. Around it are many little villages. I will [list] the villages and towns of the . . . [chief] Carlos. . . . First, a place called Tanpa, a large town, and another town which is called Tomo; and another Juchi; and another Soco; another by the name of Ño, which signifies town beloved; another Sinapa; and another Sinaesta; and another, Metampo; and another Sacalo pada; and another Calaobe; another Estame; another Yagua; another Guaya; another Yguebu; another Muspa; another Casitoa; another Tatesta; another Coyobea; another Juton; another Tequemapo; and another with the name Comachica quise; also Yobe and two other towns in that territory, the names of which I do not recollect. Besides there are others inland; on the Lake of Mayaimi; and it, Mayaimi, is the first; and another is Cutespa; another Tavagemve; another Tomsobe; another Enenpa, and there are twenty towns more whose names I do not remember. (In David O. True, *Memoir of D. d'Escalante Fontaneda Respecting Florida* [Coral Gables, Fla.: Glade House, 1945], 26–27, 51)

Guacata might well have been the name of the Fort Center village, while Tanpa was a Calusa mullet fishery at the mouth of Charlotte Harbor, the Bahía de Tanpa. Later cartographers mislocated the harbor, resulting in modern Tampa receiving its name erroneously. Juchi, a Calusa town north of Mound Key, is noted on the Freducci map, a ca. 1514–15 world map on which the depiction of Florida appears to incorporate Juan Ponce de León's discoveries. (See the map on page 136.) Tatesta is certainly the Tequesta Indians near modern Miami, whose name comes from the Indian name for Lake Okeechobee: Lake Mayaimi. The Yobe Indians gave their name to modern Hobe Sound on the Atlantic Coast. By the mid-1500s Calusa hegemony stretched across southern Florida, encompassing Glades and Belle Glade sites.

interesting. In their own way, the shellworks of this coastal culture are as extraordinary as the earthen structures of the Okeechobee Basin. And most have a Gulf-front view.

In the Caloosahatchee region, archaeological sites have a future, thanks in large part to my colleague, archaeologist William Marquardt, and the hundreds of people who participate in and support his research and efforts to preserve the archaeological heritage of the Calusa Indians and their precolumbian ancestors. Marquardt and his research team have learned a great deal that is new in the last decade and a half, and that information is being used to help manage the archaeological resources so they can be used by future generations.

The region of the post–500 B.C. Caloosahatchee culture extends from Charlotte Harbor south to the Ten Thousand Islands. This was the realm of the colonial period Calusa Indians, whose political influence was spread across south Florida, into the Lake Okeechobee Basin and all the way to the Atlantic coast.

The importance and power of the Calusa can be traced to their central political structure—that of a chiefdom—and their relatively larger and denser population, both of which were the direct result of their productive marine environment. The shallow, grassy, subtropical waters that surrounded them provided the Calusa and their ancestors with a rich larder of shellfish and fish. The Caloosahatchee people harvested the rich marine resources of Charlotte Harbor, Pine Island Sound, and San Carlos and Estero bays with their barrier and inshore islands rimmed with mangrove forests. As a consequence, they could develop a complex chiefdom based on marine resources rather than on agricultural produce.

My first visit to see firsthand Caloosahatchee shellworks sites left me in awe. The size and complexity of the site was staggering: steep shell mounds, causeways, ramps, canals, and huge middens. Not only is the size of individual sites something to behold; their collective number is also remarkable. The Caloosahatchee region features the greatest density of large shellwork sites in the United States. Almost every island and key harbors at least one such site. Some smaller islands seem to be one large site, places like Cabbage Key, Josslyn Island, Demere Key, and Mound Key. And most larger islands—Cayo Costa, North Captiva, Captiva, Sanibel, and Pine Island—are the locations of multiple mound and midden complexes. Still other sites are on the shoreline of Charlotte Harbor and on the mainland coast of Charlotte and Lee counties. Sites also are found along the Caloosahatchee River, a canoe highway connecting Caloosahatchee villages with the Belle Glade sites around Lake Okeechobee.

Some of the Caloosahatchee shell middens may first have been occupied in Late Archaic times. But even so, the accumulation of midden and the construction of mounds and ramps by the Caloosahatchee people is impressive. On Cayo Costa, for example, one shell mound is 375 feet long and 15 feet high, with smaller shell mounds built atop it. Other sites have linear middens snaking through mangrove forests for hundreds of yards. Still others have canals connecting their central portions with the inland waterways of the Gulf.

One of the most impressive Caloosahatchee construction projects is on Pine Island, where a precolumbian canal 18 to 23 feet wide and 3 to 5 feet deep was dug 2½ miles across the entire island to create a canoe shortcut from Pine Island Sound to Matlacha Pass. According to a recent study by archaeologists George Luer and Ryan Wheeler, the canal was not a sea level canal. Instead it was ingeniously engineered in stepped impoundments or segments, allowing it to cross the island's maximum elevation of 12–13 feet. Individual impoundments were dug level with small dams at each end holding in water. Travelers could simply lift their canoes across these devices, moving from a lower segment to a higher one, or vice versa, as they crossed the island in their shallow-draft dugout canoes.

The political system behind the Caloosahatchee culture and associated with the large precolumbian village-mound complexes and public works projects like the Pine Island canal was that of a centralized chiefdom. The Calusa chief and other elites, members of the chief's family, ruled the civil and religious lives of the villagers.

Why did such a complex cultural system develop on the southwest Florida coast but not on the opposite coast among Glades groups? The answer lies in intensification, using bureaucracy to maximize use of an already favorable natural environment. If we were to compare a list of plant and animal foods recovered from a Caloosahatchee site with a similar list from a Glades site, we would see few differences. But when we began to look at the relative percentages and importance of individual species and to compare various sites, we would begin to see disparities.

For instance, at some Caloosahatchee sites, sharks constitute a much larger percentage of the marine animals than at other sites, evidence that techniques were used to catch and process them en masse. Another key marine food was whelks. At one time the population of whelks on the sandy sea bottoms of the shallow bays of southwest Florida was immense.

With a single adult *Busycon* yielding nearly two pounds of meat, the millions of shells piled in middens—some of which are nearly 100 percent whelks—represent quantities of food almost beyond comprehension. By intensifying the collection of sharks and whelks and by having systems for moving food around the region, the Calusa and their ancestors could feed larger populations than could their Glades neighbors.

University of Houston archaeologist Randolph Widmer, himself a native of Florida and a renowned sport fisherman, initially assembled evidence chronicling the development of the Caloosahatchee economic and political patterns. He has suggested that optimal coastal conditions for the Caloosahatchee way of life were in place by 700 B.C., as the Late Archaic period drew to a close and sea level allowed a stable interval of estuary development. Human populations increased in number and their settlements expanded within the southwest coastal region.

By about A.D. 300, population size had led to a need for greater bureaucracy in order to manage the coastal resources more efficiently. The situation was complicated by subtle sea level fluctuations. Even slight changes could affect such things as water salinity in a favorite fishing ground, causing its abandonment by certain fish species. And higher water levels could inundate shoreline settlements. Central planning and control were needed to cope with all these situations; hereditary chiefs appeared. Chiefs controlled access to and distribution of resources, assuring that the Caloosahatchee population could continue to grow and prosper.

By A.D. 700–800, the population had reached the maximum level that the natural environment could comfortably support. Competition among villages and chiefs to control resources and people increased. An increase in the importance of chiefs is reflected in mound and shellwork construction projects that became common after this time. Village-centers can be seen at Mound Key, Big Mound Key, Galt Island, Josslyn Island, Pineland, Useppa Island, and on Sanibel Island. Powerful chiefs sought to form alliances with other groups, some of whom lived far outside Caloosahatchee territory, or they tried to annex them. Militarism increased.

The Caloosahatchee chiefs eventually extended their political sway over much of southern Florida, giving them access to more resources and allowing populations to move outside the coastal zone proper. Political complexity and centralization increased, resulting in the Calusa political system observed by Spaniards in the sixteenth century.

The power and the range of Caloosahatchee and Calusa chiefly influence is mirrored in the exchange of goods with the leaders of allied groups.

After A.D. 1000, Safety Harbor ceremonial ceramic vessels are found in Caloosahatchee mounds, perhaps a reflection of such exchanges. Then in the colonial period the cargoes salvaged from Spanish shipwrecks entered those same exchange networks. Calusa chiefs both sought to acquire such items and they distributed these new articles of wealth and status to other chiefs to cement alliances. The metal artifacts and beads found at sites like Fort Center may have been acquired by chiefs at that site in just this way.

The presence of new wealth could only have increased competition among the south Florida Indians and increased the resolve of the Calusa chiefs to control the acquisition and distribution of salvaged goods. But the invasion of people from beyond the sunrise was destined to bring far greater changes than these.

# 8    The Invasion

*Semana Santa, Pascua Florida;* Holy Week, the time of the Feast of Flowers. The exploratory expedition of Juan Ponce de León was anchored off the Atlantic coast of Florida just north of Cape Canaveral. In honor of the Easter holiday and the natural beauty of what he believed was an island, Ponce de León christened the land he saw in the distance La Florida.

It was 1513. As Christian people in Europe and the Caribbean marked the celebration of Easter, the clock began ticking down for Florida's Indians. It was the beginning of the end for the people whose ancestors had lived in Florida for more than eleven millennia. Two and a half centuries later time would end; today only a few individuals living in Louisiana can trace their ancestry to Florida's indigenous population. But even as the state's original native population was being reduced to handfuls of people, other American Indians would began to resettle the abandoned territory. This chapter and the two that follow relate the story of the Florida Indians during the nearly five centuries following Ponce de León's voyage.

Twenty-one short years before that voyage, a combination of wind, current, and luck had delivered Christopher Columbus and his small fleet to the north coast of the island of Hispaniola. In the decades following 1492, Spanish sailors, soldiers, and settlers would reach outward from that initial beachhead, founding Spanish towns first on Hispaniola and adjacent islands, even while exploring far beyond. The early voyages were carefully regulated by the Spanish crown. But the monarchs were back in Seville and undiscovered frontiers were only weeks or less away for ships out of Caribbean ports. Adventurers and slavers undoubtedly sailed well ahead of royally sanctioned voyages, leading to rumors of new lands and fortunes to be made.

Juan Ponce de León, the financially troubled ex-governor of San Juan (Puerto Rico), received a royal contract to sail northward through the Bahamas and search for a large island rumored to be in that direction. The Bahamas were well known to Spanish navigators, and it is likely that Ponce de León's initial sighting of the Florida coast was not the first by European eyes. But he was able to claim his discovery, and following his return to port, news of the Island of Florida quickly spread through the Caribbean and back to Europe.

More than a decade before that voyage, John Cabot, under an English flag, already had sailed southward down the Atlantic coast an uncertain distance below the cod fisheries off Canada's outer banks. Cabot's voyage, along with those of Ponce de León and other sailors and adventurers, led to a fierce competition among European monarchies to colonize the new land. In the end all would fail, and the new United States of America would stand victorious and in control of the Atlantic seaboard from Maine to Florida. Unfortunately for the Indians who called the huge region adjacent to the eastern seaboard home, they were caught in the chain saw of international conflict. Most coastal native peoples, like the Indians of Florida, did not survive.

Ponce de León first sighted the Florida coast near Mosquito Inlet at the southeast end of Timucua territory. He then sailed southward past the land of the Ais Indians, where native huts were sighted, perhaps fishing camps or small villages. Needing firewood and fresh water and probably anxious to see what the new land was like, Ponce sent men ashore. Skirmishes took place and two Spaniards were wounded by fish bone–tipped arrows. One Indian was kidnapped and taken to be used as a guide. The first encounters between Florida Indians and people from Europe were less than felicitous.

Continuing down the coast, Ponce de León mapped the shore and recorded natural features, naming them. He probably sailed into Biscayne Bay, where he noted the location of the main town of the Tequesta Indians at the mouth of the Miami River. Sailing farther south, he traveled along and around the Keys and then turned back north, arriving in Calusa In-

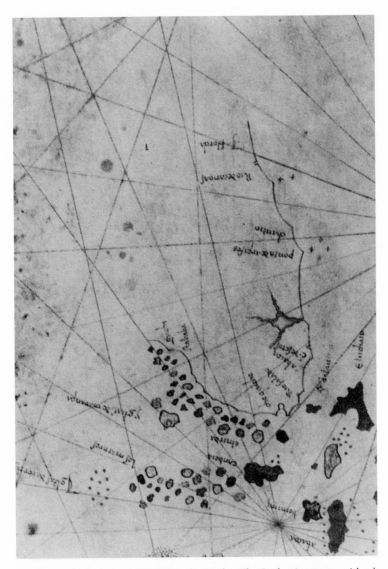

The earliest map of Florida? Florida is depicted on the Freducci map as an island. The map is thought to have been drawn in 1514–15 and lists places visited by Juan Ponce de León on his 1513 voyage. Written upside down, the Atlantic names from top to bottom are *i. florda* (Island of Florida), *Rio de canoas* (River of Canoes, probably the Indian River or Mosquito Lagoon), *chantio* (an Indian town), *ponta de arçifes* (Point of Reefs), *c. de setos* (Cape of Enclosures or Fish Weirs), *abacoa* (an Indian town), *Rio salada* (Salt River, possibly Biscayne Bay), and *chequiche* (Tequesta, the Indian town at the mouth of the Miami River). On the Gulf coast are *stababa* (Mound Key) and *guchi* (or *juchi*). The map was published in Rome in 1992 *in Atlante Colombiano della Erande Scoperta*, edited by Osvaldo Baldacci.

dian territory. Names of two Calusa towns are recorded on the Freducci map, on which the depiction of the Island of Florida is thought to be based on Ponce de León's discoveries.

The southernmost town is Stababa, called Estanapaca or Escampaba in later Spanish documents. It is certainly the archaeological site on Mound Key in Estero Bay in Lee County, the capital of the Calusa Indians in the sixteenth century. Just to the north on the same map is Guchi or Juchi, a name also mentioned in later Spanish accounts.

In Ponce de León's encounter with the Calusa Indians more skirmishes took place. The Calusa used bows and arrows to attack the Spaniards aboard their anchored ships, fighting from canoes and catamarans, canoes hooked together like the toy one recovered by Cushing from the Key Marco site. Ultimately fatalities were suffered by the Spaniards and the Calusa. Even so, both groups of combatants sought to learn more about each other and to trade in order to obtain exotic goods.

Eight years later, in 1521, Juan Ponce de León would return to Florida with a fully outfitted expedition, intending to start a colony. It is not absolutely certain, but most scholars agree that he again landed among the Calusa, this time with 200 men, Catholic clergymen, seed for planting

◇ · ◇ · ◇ · ◇ · ◇ · ◇ · ◇ · ◇ · ◇ ·

### Escampaba: A Calusa Indian Capital

In 1575, Spanish geographer López de Velasco penned this description of Estero Bay, location of Mound Key, the archaeological site that once was the capital town of the Calusa:

The Bay of Carlos, which is called Escampaba in the language of the Indians . . . appears to be the same one that is called, of Juan Ponce, because he landed in it. . . . It is at 26 ½ plus degrees [latitude; it actually is at 26 degrees 24 minutes north latitude]. Its entrance [Big Carlos Pass] is very narrow and full of shoals, as a consequence of which only [small] boats are able to enter. Within it is spacious, about four or five leagues in circumference, although all subject to flooding. There is a little island [Mound Key] in the middle that has a circumference of about a half league, with other islets around it. On this (island) Cacique Carlos had his headquarters and presently his successors have it there (as well). (Hann, *Missions to the Calusa*, 311–12)

◇ · ◇ · ◇ · ◇ · ◇ · ◇ · ◇ · ◇ · ◇ ·

crops, 50 horses, and other livestock including cows, sheep, and goats. But according to a historian of the time, his skills as a colonizer were limited at best. In renewed fighting with the Indians there were multiple fatalities. Wounded by an arrow, Ponce de León withdrew to Cuba where he soon died, probably of infection.

As word of Ponce's 1513 voyage spread, other sailors sought to explore La Florida. Sailing northward from Caribbean ports, they reconnoitered the Gulf of Mexico coast, mapping, correcting navigation charts, and capturing Indians to be sold as slaves. Already the impact of disease and maltreatment was decimating the native populations of Hispaniola and the Bahamas. More slaves were needed to fill labor needs on Hispaniola.

By 1520 the Gulf of Mexico was a Spanish sea. The entire Gulf coastline from south Florida to Yucatán was mapped, including Charlotte Harbor and Tampa Bay, though cartographers and navigators still were fine-tuning their tables of latitude to allow pinpointing of north-south locations. Voyages to the Atlantic Coast also took place, but they were fewer in number and tended to be to points north of Florida, from Amelia Island to Chesapeake Bay. Most of Florida's eastern shore was less populated than the barrier island regions of Georgia and South Carolina, and it also lacked significant harbors. Spanish slavers found easier prey elsewhere.

All of these early voyages and even the colonization attempt of Juan Ponce de León had only limited contact with Florida's Indians. What the long-term impact of those contacts was in terms of disease introduction is unknown. But the debate is moot; over the next four decades, the scene of conflict would move from the coasts to the interior of peninsular Florida, into the heartland of the Florida Indians.

### The Narváez Entrada

Spain's exploration and attempts to colonize La Florida were systematic. Often Florida endeavors were related to other initiatives in the Gulf of Mexico region. Even so, they were not always well planned, often because of a lack of knowledge about the interior of the state.

But once information was recorded about places and native people, that information was passed on and used by later Spaniards. The research I have done over the years has convinced me that the Spaniards typically retraced the same routes and revisited the same places where their predecessors had been. For instance, seventeenth-century Spaniards were well aware of where the Hernando de Soto expedition had traveled in 1539. The colonization of Florida did not occur in a vacuum.

One of the most poorly planned expeditions was that of Pánfilo de Narváez, who landed on the Gulf coast of Florida in 1528. This was the first overland Spanish expedition to encounter Florida's Indians, but it was never intended to explore peninsular Florida at all, nor did its leaders and backers ever think it would end in such disaster. The expedition had been contracted by the Spanish crown in 1526 to colonize the lands between Pánuco, a recent settlement on the northern Gulf coast of Mexico, and northwest Florida. This would provide a land link across the northernmost border of Spain's American empire. It also would lay the groundwork for an overland road from Mexico to the Atlantic coast.

Narváez was a seasoned conquistador, known for the great cruelty he had shown native people in his conquest of Cuba. The crown had high hopes. Narváez's expedition of five ships, 80 horses, and as many as 600 people, including ten women and African servants, sailed from Spain in June of 1527, making port at Santo Domingo on Hispaniola (in the modern Dominican Republic). There 140 expedition members took the opportunity to jump ship.

From Hispaniola the expedition sailed west to Cuba to secure more supplies. Then ships were sent to Trinidad to garner more supplies. There two storms struck, one perhaps a hurricane, drowning 60 people and 20 horses. Finally in February of 1528, the reunited expedition of 400 sailors and colonists set sail, only to run aground almost immediately. After more delays, the small fleet again sailed, heading northward toward its goal, the northern Gulf of Mexico coast.

On April 12, nearly two months after slipping anchor in Cuba, they finally sighted the Gulf coast. But Narváez was nowhere near his goal. Because supplies were low, he opted to anchor and go ashore. Unfortunately for the expedition's members, the charts used by the pilot, Diego de Miruelo, still reflected latitudinal errors that indicated places to be a degree and a half—about 90 miles—farther north than they actually were. I and others believe that Juan Ponce de León had similar erroneous data when he sailed fifteen years earlier.

As luck would have it, Narváez's ships had anchored off the coast of Pinellas County, west of the north end of Tampa Bay. A party sent ashore to explore soon came upon the bay as well as a village of the Tocobaga Indians. There, probably near the modern town of Safety Harbor, the Spaniards saw goods the Tocobaga had salvaged from wrecked Spanish ships.

Trusting his erroneous navigation tables, Narváez was convinced that the bay he had found was the southernmost peninsular Florida harbor—Charlotte Harbor—and that farther to the north would be another, even better harbor, Tampa Bay. Accordingly, he decided to take most of his men and set out overland, marching to the northern harbor. Native guides had taken him 10–12 leagues north of Tampa Bay to a village where there was corn; agricultural produce would be used to feed his army as it marched north.

Earlier, one ship had been sent back to Cuba to report and to bring more supplies. But by the time that ship returned, Narváez already had departed. Before he left, however, he had ordered his other ships to sail north, find the (nonexistent) northern harbor, and wait there. Because there was no northern harbor, the land expedition would find only disaster.

On its return, the ship sent to Cuba landed four men at Tampa Bay to search for some sign of the expedition. When the men were attacked by Indians, their shipmates quickly decided to leave them to their fate, hoisting anchor and sailing back to Cuba. It was one of those Spaniards, Juan Ortiz, who would live among the Tampa Bay Indians for 11 years before being found in 1539 by the de Soto expedition.

The ships sent up the coast to look for the missing harbor spent a fruitless year before giving up. By that time, only a handful of the original members of the land expedition were still alive, living with Indians in coastal Texas. Eventually those few survivors would make their way to Mexico. Later one of them, Alvar Núñez Cabeza de Vaca, would travel back to Spain, where he wrote the story of what had befallen the ill-fated expedition.

As it turned out, 300 men—the women had departed on the ships—had marched north from Tampa Bay toward the nonexistent harbor. Along the journey, the army maintained several miles between itself and the soggy coastline. This route apparently took the expedition between the Safety Harbor people living directly on the coast and those living inland, for instance in the Cove of the Withlacoochee. As a consequence, few Indians were seen until the Spaniards crossed the Withlacoochee River and encountered as many as 200 people. Several Indians were taken hostage and made to guide the army to their village, where corn was found and where the Spaniards rested for a week.

Soldiers were sent downriver to the coast, in hopes that the river led into the missing harbor, but it did not. The army, rested and with captive

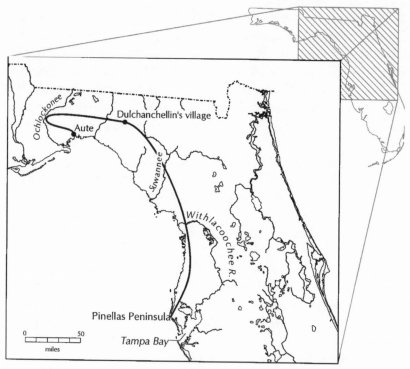

Route of the 1528 Pánfilo de Narváez expedition from northern Tampa Bay to northwest Florida

Indian guides, again marched north. Somewhere in Dixie County they were met by a Timucuan chief named Dulchanchellin, who had heard of the Spaniards and had come from his village in Madison County to greet them.

The chief was attired in a painted deerskin and was carried on the shoulders of his people, probably in a litter. Accompanying him were other villagers, who announced his presence by playing reed flutes. He let the Spaniards know he was an enemy of the Apalachee Indians, toward whose territory they were headed, and he enticed them to come to his village. Most likely the chief had plans to include the Spaniards and their superior weapons in an attack on the Apalachee. The Spaniards followed Dulchanchellin north, crossing the Suwannee River before arriving at his village, where they were fed corn. It seems certain that they were in the main village of the Yustaga Indians, also later visited by de Soto.

The expedition next headed west across the Aucilla River into Apalachee. I believe their captive guides—probably Apalachee Indians—intentionally led them through the roughest landscape they could find, staying away from villages where the Spaniards might have found supplies. The army probably was guided through San Pedro Bay—a swamp—and then led all of the way to the Ochlockonee River.

Eventually the Spaniards made camp in a small village in a little-populated locale, where they stayed for more than three weeks, suffering from hunger and the wounds caused by chafing armor. Scouting parties failed to find native towns with stored foods that could be taken. Indian hostages told Narváez that corn, beans, and squashes could be found in a town called Aute near the coast. Once again the Spaniards were cleverly steered away from the Apalachee heartland and the large Fort Walton towns in Leon and Jefferson counties.

Breaking camp, the Spaniards set out on a lengthy eight- or nine-day march to reach Aute. Along the way they were constantly harassed by native archers. In Aute, probably on the St. Marks River, they found food. A scouting party was sent to find the coast. Narváez, thoroughly lost and realizing that his expedition had little chance of accomplishing its objectives, intended to walk along the Gulf shore to reach Mexico.

At Aute about a third of the expedition's members became ill, hastening a decision to move to the coast. On the march to the coast, some men simply deserted. Once there, Narváez instituted a change of plans: It would be impossible for the army to march along the swampy coast all of the way to Mexico. Instead, the Spaniards would build rafts, outfit them as best they could, and travel by water. Using makeshift bellows and other equipment, the soldiers forged horse tack and weapons into nails and tools. In a month and a half, five rafts were built and caulked with palmetto fiber and pine pitch. During that time the men ate their horses, fashioning the hides into water bags and weaving manes and tails into rope.

Just over five months after they first had sighted La Florida, the army, down to about 250 people, floated into oblivion. Eleven years later, men from de Soto's expedition would find Narváez's coastal camp. But by then the expedition's four survivors had made their way to Mexico and told their story. Their companions had all disappeared, most carried out into the Gulf to die, although a few might have still been living among Indians, having been captured when some of the rafts washed ashore.

Future expeditions learned three things from the Narváez disaster: planning was everything, colonizing La Florida was not going to be easy, and the Indians of La Florida were clever and formidable. But rather than discouraging future exploration, the Narváez catastrophe actually encouraged more attempts at colonization. The stories told by the survivors—one of whom was a black Moorish slave, Estebanico—quickly spread, no doubt embellished in the retelling. The rumors of golden cities to the north of Mexico would entice Francisco Coronado and others to march north out of that Spanish colony searching for Eldorado.

### Hernando de Soto

By August 1537, the single Narváez expedition survivor who had traveled back to Spain was telling people there of his extraordinary adventure. As one of the de Soto chroniclers wrote, the stories he related led people to believe that La Florida was the richest land in the world. The tales were a help to the recruiting efforts of Hernando de Soto, another seasoned conquistador who had made a fortune looting and slaving in Central and South America. De Soto himself was putting together an expedition to colonize the lands north and east of Mexico all the way to Florida and the Atlantic coast.

In April of 1538, de Soto's expedition sailed from Spain for the Caribbean. His state-of-the art military and colonial venture included soldiers as well as craftsmen and people to build forts and towns. Gentleman soldiers traveled with squires, extra horses, and spare weaponry, and everyone of noble class took servants and packed trunks of clothes, tents, field furnishings, dishware, and serving items. This would be Spain's most ambitious initiative to conquer La Florida. But it, too, ultimately would be defeated by the land and its people.

The fleet sailed first to Cuba, where de Soto claimed its governorship, as granted by his royal contact. In Cuba he set up the administrative and logistic support for his expedition and for his future Florida colony. Scout ships, armed with corrected sea charts and knowledge of Narváez's errors, reconnoitered the peninsular Gulf coast and found Tampa Bay, then known as Bahía Honda.

In mid-May of 1539, the expedition of five large and four smaller ships sailed. A week later the fleet anchored off Longboat Key and over the next several days moved into Tampa Bay, where de Soto set up camp in the main village of the Uzita Indians on the Little Manatee River. There were unloaded 750 people, including women (two of whom would join the overland expedition; the others returned to Cuba), tailors, shoemakers, a stocking maker, a notary, blacksmith, trumpeter, servants, clergy, cavalry, infantry, attack dogs, 220 horses, a drove of pigs, and supplies for 18 months. Four years later, 310 poorly armed men and one woman, all in rags, would leave La Florida. Behind them they would leave everything and everyone else, including de Soto.

If nothing else, de Soto was cautious. During his first six weeks in La Florida, he sent out armed parties to learn about the landscape, the native people, and the potential of the two to support an army on the move. De Soto's plan was to feed his traveling colonists and soldiers from the stored foodstuffs of the Indians. He also intended to use native people as bearers and as consorts for his men. Flexing their military might, the Spaniards would appropriate food and people as needed.

De Soto realized that it was in his best interests not to antagonize his hosts or the other native groups around Tampa Bay, people like the Mocoso Indians. But that was not always possible, and the soldiers did not hesitate to exert force to ensure obedience. Communication with the Tampa Bay Indians was made easier by the presence of Juan Ortiz, the Spaniard who had been captured while searching for Narváez in 1528.

Convinced that he could live off the land, de Soto made the decision to head northward toward the land of the Ocale Indians, where he was led to believe he would find significant amounts of stored food. There he planned to spend the winter. But rather than putting all his eggs in one basket, de Soto left more than 100 people and a large amount of supplies behind in Uzita's village. With him were about 500 Spaniards and at least several hundred Indians—perhaps many more—who carried the expedition's supplies and equipment. Some of the ships also were left at Tampa Bay; others were sent back to Cuba.

Their path took the Spaniards across the Manatee and Alafia rivers, up the east side of Tampa Bay, and then farther north to the Cove of the Withlacoochee River. As they marched through the Safety Harbor region led by captive Indian guides, they traveled east of Narváez's route along established trails. A group of cavalry and infantry was sent farther inland to see firsthand what the Timucua Indians living west of modern Orlando, at the southern end of the central lake district, might offer in terms of wealth and food, but those soldiers returned to rejoin the main army.

Even though the native guides were threatened with having limbs cut off or being thrown to attack dogs—punishments often administered—they deliberately led de Soto to the east side of the large wetland known today as the Cove of the Withlacoochee and duped him into believing that the only way to reach the main village of the Ocale Indians on the opposite side was to cross the swamp, a trip of several days. Years after, some of the expedition members still remembered the hardships incurred in that

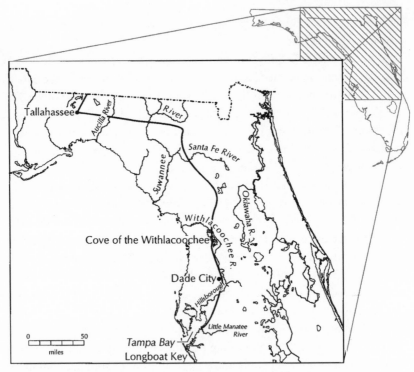

Route taken by the Hernando de Soto expedition from lower Tampa Bay to
Apalachee in 1539

crossing. A much easier route would have been simply to bypass the Cove,
traveling around its northern end.

The Ocale Indian town in southwest Sumter County was a disappoint-
ment. The food de Soto had been led to believe would be there could feed
the hungry army for only a few days. Though they did grow corn, the
Ocale were not intensive farmers; their stored food supplies could not long
feed hundreds of hungry Spaniards. De Soto began to implement plan B.
First, men were sent farther east to the Acuera Indians, another Timucuan
group in the Oklawaha River drainage or slightly farther south. There
stored corn supplies were taken and brought back to Ocale, probably forcibly transported by Indians in chains.

But even Ocale and Acuera combined, together with the surrounding
countryside, could not support the army all winter. De Soto went to plan
C. He would march rapidly north with 50 cavalry and 60 infantry to locate
better winter quarters, while the rest of the army waited at Ocale, living as
best they could by raiding the countryside. Though it was as yet early Au-

gust, de Soto did not known when winter might begin or how harsh it might be.

From Ocale this advance party marched north through Marion and Alachua counties, through Potano Indian territory, before crossing the Santa Fe River into western Columbia County. There, in northern Utina territory at the Timucuan village of Aguacaleyquen, de Soto found himself in a more densely populated region, the home of Suwannee Valley culture farmers. Badly outnumbered, de Soto grabbed the village chief's daughter as a hostage and sent horseman back to Ocale with orders for the remainder of the army to join him at Aguacaleyquen, which they did. Once the army was reunited and ready to move, the chief himself was taken hostage, further insurance against attacks.

Intelligence gathered from the Indians led de Soto to conclude that Apalachee might be a suitable wintering place, although he well knew what had befallen Narváez there. The army turned westward across northern Florida, heading for Apalachee. It was a gamble, but de Soto knew he still had his ships and reserve force at Tampa Bay.

In western Suwannee County two fierce battles were fought against Timucua Indians. The Indians suffered heavy casualties, including the execution of several hundred warriors and nearly a dozen village chiefs. It was standard policy for the Spaniards to counter any show of opposition with massive and cruel force. Seventy years after the army marched through Potano Indian territory, one village chief, a boy in 1539, still remembered the brutality of de Soto and refused to interact with Franciscan friars.

Crossing the Suwannee River into Madison County brought the army into the territory of the Yustaga Indians, the Timucuan group whose chief Dulchanchellin had helped Narváez. A new chief, Chief Uzachile, had sent peaceful overtures to de Soto even before the army reached the Suwannee River. But when the Spaniards arrived at the main Yustaga village, they found it abandoned. The Yustaga had learned all about conquistadors from their encounter with Narváez and opted this time simply to withdraw, taking their food and leaving the Spaniards with no option but to press forward.

The Apalachee would not yield as peacefully. From the time de Soto arrived at the eastern edge of their territory—the Aucilla River—the Apalachee employed guerilla tactics to harass the army. After several days, despite attempts by hostage guides to mislead them, the army arrived at Iniahica, the Apalachee capital at the time. Lake Jackson apparently had

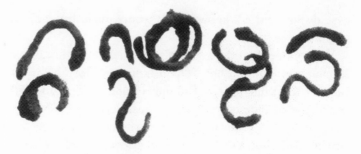

De Soto's chain mail? These tiny, twisted bits of metal, the largest of which are less than an inch long, were excavated from the site of Iniahica, where the de Soto expedition wintered in 1539–40. Discovered by archaeologist B. Calvin Jones, Iniahica is within sight of Florida's capitol building in Tallahassee.

been abandoned earlier. The journey through Apalachee made two things abundantly clear to the Spaniards: the agricultural bounty of the Apalachee could support the army over the winter, but the Apalachee themselves would not give up their property easily. It was early October when de Soto commandeered Iniahica for his winter camp.

The Indians living between Tampa Bay and Apalachee who had suffered the army's march northward from Tampa Bay to Apalachee must have been dismayed at what happened next. A contingent of cavalry was sent back along the same route to Uzita's village at Tampa Bay with orders to break camp. Most of the people left there were to march to Iniahica, again tracing de Soto's route. The ships anchored at Tampa Bay would be used to bring the remaining people camped there and the supplies up the coast, where they would be off-loaded and taken overland to Iniahica. Then the ships were to explore the coast.

The plan worked to perfection. In March 1540, de Soto's army, resupplied and more than 500 strong, broke camp and marched into Georgia and northwestern South Carolina before turning northwesterly across the Appalachian Mountains into Tennessee. Not finding the wealth he sought, de Soto then headed southwest into Alabama. At one point he had the option of continuing to the Gulf coast near Mobile, but he turned back north, arriving in Mississippi, where the army spent the winter of 1540–41.

It was a bad decision. The mineral wealth de Soto sought did not exist. Nor would it be found in Arkansas, where the army spent nearly a year after having crossed the Mississippi River in May of 1541. Returning to camp on the river the next year, de Soto became ill and died in June. Dispirited, the army turned toward survival, first trying to walk across Texas to Mexico, then returning to the Mississippi River a third time to build boats, in which the survivors intended to float downriver to the Gulf and proceed to Mexico. A year after de Soto's death, the survivors reached the Gulf of Mexico; two and a half months later, they reached a Spanish settlement near Tampico, Mexico, ending an incredible odyssey.

The impact of the de Soto entrada on the Indians of the Southeast is still being debated. In Florida it is certain that impact was immense: lives lost, diseases introduced, villages decimated, stored foods stolen, and populations scattered. The Indians of eastern and southern Tampa Bay, the Uzita and Mocoso, never recovered; the entire district around Ocale must have been similarly devastated. Along the route the entrada took from Tampa Bay to Apalachee—not once but three times—the immediate impact must have been horrendous.

### Another Attempt

The failure of the de Soto expedition shook Spain. How could such a successful conquistador have come to such an end? Ponce, Narváez, and now de Soto—all had failed to establish the La Florida colony that would secure the Spanish empire's northern border. The cost in Spanish lives had been great. As a result, the crown essentially established a moratorium on future attempts.

But 15 years later, the realities of international competition for the eastern United States would lead to still another unsuccessful colonization attempt, one that revived the plan for a road from Mexico to Santa Elena on the South Carolina portion of the Atlantic coast. To maintain a road, Spanish settlements were needed on the upper Gulf coast as well as on the Atlantic coast at Santa Elena. Goods from Mexico could be transported on the road, loaded aboard ships at Santa Elena, and shipped to Spain, avoiding the often dangerous route around the Gulf of Mexico coast and through the Florida Straits, a route that had claimed treasure-laden ships in the past. Settlements along the road would support missions ministering to the native population, turning potentially hostile Indians into Christians, who presumably would act favorably toward Spanish interests.

And the specter persisted of great wealth still to be found and fortunes to be made. Despite the realities witnessed firsthand by the de Soto expedition, there still were rumors of a land of milk and honey with resources for the taking, a land called Chicora, somewhere in the interior of the Carolinas.

For all these reasons, a new expedition was contracted. The first settlement was planned for Ochuse, an Indian town in Pensacola Bay that had been visited earlier by de Soto's ships. Unlike previous attempts at colonization, this one, sponsored by the viceroy of Mexico, Luís de Velasco, and led by Tristán de Luna y Arellano, would sail from Veracruz on the Gulf coast of Mexico. After some problems, the fleet of 13 ships carrying 1,500 people—including Indians from Mexico and an Indian woman taken to Mexico by de Soto's army—found the correct harbor and landed.

In August of 1559, the bay was renamed Bahía Filipina del Puerto de Santa María, though the colonists often called their settlement Polonza, perhaps an Indian name. Disaster struck almost immediately. Nine ships, some still loaded, were sunk in a hurricane, leaving the colonists without most of their supplies. Several unsuccessful attempts were made to move colonists inland to live off food taken from Indians. Groups of people were sent all the way into northeastern Alabama, but the Indians who had been living there at the time of de Soto were gone, perhaps having withdrawn at the approach of another Spanish expedition.

With the colony in desperate shape and many of its members in open rebellion against Luna, who was ill and suffering mental duress, ships arrived from Mexico in April of 1561 to remove the colonists to Santa Elena. But most had had enough. At a stopover in Havana, many opted out. Several of the ships that continued to the Atlantic coast were lost in a storm, and the others soon turned back. Ochuse and Santa Elena would be two more failures.

### The French and Fort Caroline

France, Spain's rival for La Florida, was well aware of these latest attempts at colonization. In early 1562, the French crown would send its own expedition to La Florida. Led by Jean Ribault, the 150-person entrada landed near St. Augustine and then sailed north to the mouth of the St. Johns River, where the land was claimed for France and a stone marker erected. While there, Ribault encountered Timucua Indians who exchanged goods with him as a show of friendship and respect, although their chiefs refused to render obedience to the French soldier.

Ribault sailed on northward, exploring the coasts of Georgia and South Carolina before founding a fort at Santa Elena, christened Charlesfort. France, in one swift stroke, had usurped Spanish claims. Ribault returned to France to report, leaving a portion of his soldiers at the fort.

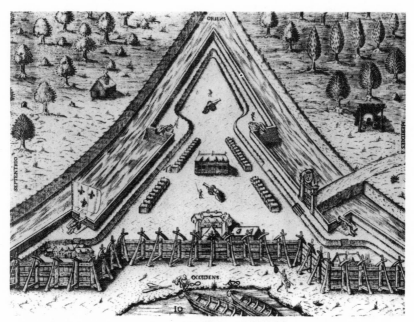
Fort Caroline, as engraved by Theodore de Bry in 1591 based on French accounts

The fort would soon be abandoned when its poorly supplied and hungry soldiers manned a small boat and made their way back to France in an arduous journey across the Atlantic. But word that France was making inroads in La Florida already had reached the Spanish court, and plans to counter what was viewed as French aggression were being considered.

In the meanwhile, a second French expedition was being readied to sail. Led by René de Laudonnière—who had been second in command under Ribault in 1562—300 colonists, including men and women settlers, soldiers, and craftsmen, made landfall on the Florida Atlantic coast in July 1564.

Accompanying Laudonnière was Jacques Le Moyne, a cartographer and artist who later would paint a series of watercolors depicting the Florida Timucua Indians. Although only one still exists today, the paintings were used by Theodore de Bry, one of a family of German engravers and publishers, as the basis for illustrations in a book published in 1591 in Frankfurt on the French colonial efforts in La Florida. The de Bry engravings of the Le Moyne paintings remain an often-cited source on the Florida Indians, though today we realize that de Bry borrowed liberally from illustrations of South American Indians.

Laudonnière sailed into the mouth of the St. Johns River and relocated Ribault's marker. After exploring upriver for a short distance and then scouting the coast to the north, the French returned and began work on Fort Caroline on the south bank of the St. Johns River.

By mid-fall supplies were dwindling and discontent had set in. The colonists quickly learned to barter with the local Timucua Indians for food, even trading their clothes for corn, beans, acorns, fish, deer, turkeys, and other game. With the hungry French at their mercy, Indians traveled great distances to strike hard bargains.

◇ · ◇ · ◇ · ◇ · ◇ · ◇ · ◇ · ◇ · ◇

## French Fort Caroline

René de Laudonnière would return to France and write a narrative of his adventures in Florida, including a description of Fort Caroline. Today the National Park Service operates the Fort Carolina National Monument. It is well worth the trip to the south bank of the St. Johns River to visit the museum and the full-size reproduction of the fort.

The only problem is that as yet, not a single shred of physical evidence for the original fort has been found. Since the 1940s historians and archaeologists have searched, to no avail, for remains matching Laudonnière's description:

> Our fort was built in a triangular shape. The west side, which was the landward side, was bounded by a little ditch and built with turfs [sod] making a parapet nine feet high. The other side [north], which was toward the river, was bounded by a timber palisade. . . . On the south side there was a kind of bastion, inside which I had a supply shed built. The whole thing was built of stakes and sand, except for about two or three feet of turf, of which the parapets were made. I had a large area eighteen paces square made in the middle. In the center of that, facing the southern side, I had a guardhouse built, and a house on the other, northern side. I built it a bit too high, for not long afterwards the wind blew it down. . . . I had an oven [for baking] built at some distance from the fort to avoid the risk of fire, since the houses were covered with palm leaves. (Sarah Lawson and John W. Faupel, eds., *A Foothold in Florida: The Eye-Witness Account of Four Voyages Made by the French to That Region* [East Grimstead, Eng.: Antique Atlas Publications, 1992], 60–62)

◇ · ◇ · ◇ · ◇ · ◇ · ◇ · ◇ · ◇ · ◇

Chief Outina leads his warriors and French soldiers against Chief Potano in this highly speculative engraving. Indian warfare in Florida never featured attacking phalanxes of warriors.

After only a short time in Florida, the French undertook a number of initiatives to explore the land and try to secure food for their survival. They traveled the lower St. Johns River valley north of Lake George, the heartland of the eastern Timucuan tribes, and they had many dealings with the Timucua Indians living north of the river mouth. French soldiers also were sent across the entire expanse of Timucuan territory west to the Yustaga Indians. However, their most intense contact, not surprisingly, was with nearby Timucuan Indians, all from villages that were part of an alliance headed by Chief Saturiwa, who lived near the fort.

But the Timucua Indians around Fort Caroline were not intensive agriculturists, and they did not have surpluses of corn that the French could take. The local residents, like their precolumbian ancestors, lived mainly by fishing, hunting, and collecting wild foods; they grew crops but not to the extent that the Timucua living farther inland did.

As a consequence, the French were forced to look to other Timucua for significant amounts of corn. Farther south on the St. Johns River was another Timucuan alliance, headed by Chief Outina, an alliance that apparently stretched south to Lake George. By befriending Outina, Laudonnière sought to gain access to corn grown in that region. Outina was well aware of the colonists' position and sought to turn the situation to his own advantage. Twice, in 1564 and in early 1565, he cajoled the French into providing soldiers armed with arquebuses to accompany him and his warriors in attacks on the main village of the Potano Indians, his enemies.

By the late spring of 1565, the French were again suffering from food shortages. The nearby corn crops were not ripe and Outina refused to provide corn or beans, explaining that what he had was needed for seed. To force French demands, Chief Outina was taken hostage and held for a ransom of food, which the Indians said they could not pay. After two tense weeks of skirmishes and one all-out battle, Outina was released.

In August an English ship stopped off at Fort Caroline and agreed to trade food and supplies for French armaments. Resupplied, Laudonnière ordered preparations to return to France. As luck would have it, at nearly the exact moment the French ships were to depart at the end of the month, Jean Ribault appeared with a small fleet, more supplies, and orders to take over the colony.

But La Florida would not remain long in French hands. Hot on Ribault's heels was a Spanish fleet captained by Pedro Menéndez de Avilés, sent from Spain to oust the French and establish a Spanish colony. Over the next two months, operating from a fortified encampment that the Spanish christened St. Augustine, Menéndez used a combination of naval and land operations to remove the French presence and take over Fort Caroline. Aided by a storm that scattered and wrecked Jean Ribault's fleet, Menéndez crushed the French. His murder of a number of French Protestant soldiers who surrendered to him is still controversial today.

Having established a toehold in Florida, Menéndez would set about securing and expanding Spain's hold on the land and the Indians who lived there. Florida would be a Spanish colony for the next two centuries.

# 9   Spanish Missions and the Impact of Colonialism

One of my favorite historical sites to visit in Florida is the Castillo de San Marcos, the massive stone fort in St. Augustine maintained for the public by the National Park Service. I like the cool dampness that emanates from the thick coquina walls of the interior rooms. Less enticing are the pungent odors of more than three centuries of soldiers, prisoners, workers, and, more recently one supposes, tourists.

I always marvel at the contrast between this fort, a symbol of colonial power, and the Spanish mission sites that I have visited or excavated. Ironically, the latter were homes to many of the several hundred Indians who were forced to labor in the construction of the fort in the 1670s.

The best way to envision a mission site is to look out of the window while driving along a rural north Florida road. Sometimes one sees woods, sometimes pasture, but never a Spanish mission. That is exactly what a Spanish mission looks like today: nothing. Forts were built of stone; missions were built of wood and clay. Seventeenth-century missions were not built to last, and none survived long in the Florida climate. Seventeenth-century forts still stand and are visited by thousands of people every year. Yet mission sites, too, are symbols of power. Their fragile construction relative to the stone castillo in St. Augustine reflects the unequal social, political, and military relationships between the Florida Indians and the Spanish crown, represented in Florida by the officials and soldiers of the Florida colony centered in St. Augustine.

Toss in the tragic results of unintentionally introduced diseases and the military conflicts among colonial powers that often entangled the native people and used them as pawns, and one can only conclude that the indigenous residents of Florida never had a chance. Despite the best intentions of Jesuit priests and Franciscan friars, Florida's Indians would not survive the events of the two centuries between 1565 and 1763; the many concessions and cultural changes they implemented could not withstand the new social and biological environment that enveloped them.

The story of the Florida missions begins in the early fall of 1565, when Pedro Menéndez de Avilés set about consolidating Spain's tenuous hold on La Florida. High on his list was securing its coasts and assuring the colony access to an excellent harbor and to sea lanes. Menéndez was a sea captain; the colony of La Florida would be supported and protected by ships that could sail its inland waterways and the surrounding oceans.

Menéndez had ambitious plans. The colony's main town would not be at St. Augustine but at Santa Elena on the South Carolina coast, where Ribault had built Charlesfort, abandoned three years earlier. From Santa Elena the Spaniards could build their long-sought overland road to northern Mexico.

Another initiative was to discover the rumored northwest passage, a sea lane across northern North America connecting the Atlantic and Pacific oceans. A possible entry to this passage was thought to be in Chesapeake Bay. Controlling such a waterway would give Spain direct access to the riches of the Asian East. Santa Elena would play a key role in the ensuing sea commerce.

One way to protect the coasts of La Florida was to establish garrisons and missions. Missions would be staffed by Jesuits under an agreement Menéndez had with that religious order. Garrison-mission settlements would be established near the mouths of several Florida rivers, all of which were thought to be interconnected. The rivers would be an intra-Florida highway uniting Spanish settlements.

The proposed Spanish outposts would be among the Tocobaga Indians at Tampa Bay near the Hillsborough River, the Calusa near the Caloosahatchee River, the Tequesta at the Miami River, and the Timucua at the mouth of the St. Johns River near Fort Caroline, reoccupied and renamed San Mateo by the Spaniards. Still other outposts would be established at

Tocobaga

St. Augustine

St. Johns River

Hillsborough River

Lake Okeechobee

Caloosahatchee

Escampaba

Miami River

Tequesta

0 ——————— 100

miles

Pedro Menéndez's erroneous conception of Florida's
river system, which he hoped to use to secure the
peninsula

St. Lucie Inlet and on Cumberland Island, Georgia, both on the Atlantic
coast, and one would be on Chesapeake Bay.

Converting the Florida Indians to Catholicism was an important part
of Menéndez's plan for Florida as well as a requirement of his royal contract. Christian Indians would be made into loyal subjects of the Spanish
crown and supporters of the colony. Not only would there be Jesuit missions; there would be a Jesuit school in Havana to educate the native des-
ignees of Florida's Indian chiefs. Youths would be introduced to Hispanic
culture and then returned to Florida, where they would assume their status as chiefs, ensuring many generations of loyal native leaders.

Over the decade following the defeat of the French, Menéndez set about
making these plans a reality. Had he been successful, the history of North
America would have had a very different outcome. But instead, every one
of the initiatives failed.

Santa Elena was indeed established as St. Augustine's sister city. But it never became the capital of the colony as intended; inertia conspired against it. Menéndez and others could not convince the colonists in St. Augustine to abandon that town and move north. By 1587, Santa Elena was abandoned.

The overland trail to Mexico was never built. The Spaniards' belief that the Appalachian Mountains extended to Mexico only a relatively short distance away was erroneous; Mexico was much more distant than they thought. Finding a northwest passage also never happened; from the beginning it was a figment of geographical misinformation. I believe that the rumor was the result of wishful thinking by Europeans and misinterpretation of stories related by Indians about the Great Lakes. The lakes certainly were large bodies of water, but they were not the Pacific Ocean that Europeans sought. An inland Florida waterway was likewise based on erroneous understanding of native information. Dugout canoes and native rowers willing to portage might have been able to travel the web of water in interior Florida, but Spanish ships could not.

Coastal garrisons and missions, some served by resident Jesuit priests, were established, but none lasted more than a few years. For a short time the Jesuits looked toward the Georgia and South Carolina coasts—the region between St. Augustine and Santa Elena—for mission converts, but those attempts also failed, and in 1572 the order withdrew from Florida.

Later in that year or early in the next, Menéndez secured agreements that opened Florida to Franciscan friars. By the end of 1573, Father Francisco del Castillo, a Franciscan, was ministering in Santa Elena. Several years later Father Alonso Cavezas was in St. Augustine, although both probably served the Spanish garrisons stationed in each town rather than Indian missions.

The death of Menéndez in 1574 sealed the fate of his plans for expanding Spanish settlements north and west from Santa Elena and St. Augustine. It would be Franciscan friars, representatives of the church and the colonial government of La Florida, who sowed and cultivated the seeds of Catholicism and Castile, as Spain was most often called at the time. Franciscans would spread Christianity and Spanish influence all across northern Florida to the Apalachicola River and into southern Georgia.

In Florida the primary sphere of the missions was among the Timucua and Apalachee Indians. At various times missions were attempted among other peoples, such as San Salvador de Mayaca among the Mayaca Indians south of Lake George on the St. Johns River. But none of the outlying missions lasted for long.

Because the Apalachee and Timucua Indians and the Guale in coastal Georgia were farmers, it was among them that missions would achieve their greatest successes. In large part this was a self-fulfilling prophesy: colonial and church authorities emphasized missionizing farmers. That was because the colony would depend heavily on agricultural produce, especially corn, to feed itself. Missions among farming populations made it easier to use native labor to produce and process corn and transport it to St. Augustine. Labor drafts could be organized through mission villages and their native chiefs. Use of conscripted Indian labor to fill the colony's needs in St. Augustine and in the mission provinces also could be instituted through the missions.

As a result, it is safe to say that La Florida's very existence was built atop the Apalachee and Timucua Indians, as well as the Guale, who became harnessed to the colony through the missions. The missions and the new diseases introduced from Europe would have far-reaching impacts on the cultures of the northern Florida Indians, turning them into Catholic subjects of the crown and, eventually, decimating them.

The plan for establishing missions was as follows. Within the main town of each Indian chiefdom there would be a *doctrina*, a mission with a church and a resident priest who instructed the native people in religious matters, the doctrine. Chiefdoms with several large towns would receive more missions, although some towns initially might have *visitas*, missions visited by a friar from a nearby doctrina, rather than a full-time resident friar. Apalachee, with its large population and many towns, would require many missions. The first missions would be along the coast between St. Augustine and Santa Elena, in Timucua and Guale villages. But with the abandonment of Santa Elena by 1587, the Franciscan coastal mission chain never extended farther north than St. Catherine's Island and the Ogeechee and Midway rivers on the Georgia coast.

Staffing of the planned missions began in 1584, when eight friars left Spain for Florida. They were to be the vanguard of the Franciscan effort among the Florida Indians. But the initial results were less than satisfactory. Only four friars actually arrived in Florida—the others had stayed in ports along the way. A fifth soon left Florida for Mexico. Twelve more friars arrived in 1587 and another eight in 1590. But two years later, only two friars and a lay brother remained; life in Florida was a challenge.

In 1595 another group of 12 friars arrived in St. Augustine and implementation of the plans for the mission system finally could begin in earnest. Within a year, ten doctrinas were functioning, nine of which were from St. Augustine northward along the coast among the Timucua and Guale Indians. The tenth (San Antonio de Enecape) was at the Timucuan village of Enecape, the Mt. Royal archaeological site just north of Lake George. From San Pedro de Mocamo on Cumberland Island, Georgia, Father Baltasar López traveled far into the interior of northern Florida to seek conversions among the Potano and northern Utina Indians, laying the groundwork for future missions in that region.

In 1597 a major setback occurred when a rebellion by the Guale Indians resulted in the destruction of their missions and the deaths of five friars. The Guale chain of missions north of St. Simons Island would gradually be rebuilt.

Surprisingly, not a single one of these early missions was within the St. Johns drainage from its mouth all the way to the Mt. Royal site, the large region once the home of the people of the Saturiwa and Outina alliances. It appears that epidemics introduced during the 1562–95 period of contact with the French and then the Spaniards had effectively decimated the Timucua population of the area.

In 1606, a second chain of missions was started well west of St. Augustine among the Timucua chiefdoms of interior northern Florida and southern Georgia, where Father López had traveled. But again, no missions were located from St. Augustine all the way to Potano territory, a reflection of the massive depopulation that had occurred around St. Augustine for many miles. On several occasions during the seventeenth century, the Spaniards would move Indians to new mission villages within that area—for instance, to where the main road from St. Augustine crossed the St. Johns River, so that they could operate a ferry. But the indigenous Indians were gone.

The first mission among the Potano was San Francisco de Potano, quickly followed by three others. Some of these earliest interior missions did not have a resident friar. But by 1612 epidemics had severely reduced the number of Potano, and two of the missions already had been abandoned. Over the next 20 years, missions were systematically founded in each of the other interior Timucuan chiefdoms, beginning in modern Columbia, Suwannee, and Madison counties. The largest number of missions were in Yustaga, where the population was greatest at the time.

Missions were connected to one another along the web of crossing trails, use of which reached well back into precolumbian times. A few missions were accessible by a combination of land and canoe travel. Distances to some were so great that friars and Spanish officials complained about how far one had to travel west from St. Augustine and then north or south to reach them.

The name given each mission reflected both the saint's day or holy day on which mass was first held there and the name of the Indian village or place where the mission was located. For instance, San Juan de Guacara in southern Suwannee County near the Suwannee River was named for St. John and Guacara, the Timucuan name for the Suwannee River; San Francisco de Potano was named after St. Francis and the town or Indians of Potano; and San Pedro y San Pablo de Potohiriba near Lake Sampala in Madison County was named for St. Peter and St. Paul and the Yustaga village of Potohiriba (San Pablo is the basis for the name Sampala).

In 1633, with the Florida Timucua essentially all living in villages served by friars, efforts were shifted to the Apalachee Indians west of the Aucilla River. Already Franciscan friars had visited the region. Apalachee would be a coup for the Spaniards. Its productive Indian farmers could supply St. Augustine with significant amounts of corn and other food. A disadvantage was its long distance from St. Augustine, but Indian bearers taken from the villages of Apalachee and Timucua were made to transport corn and other goods on their backs. The journey could be made somewhat easier by carrying corn to the Suwannee River, canoeing it downstream to the Santa Fe River, and then proceeding up the Santa Fe River to the natural bridge (today in O'Leno State Park). From there it could be carried overland the rest of the way to St. Augustine.

Still another route from Apalachee was via the back door: from the St. Marks River to the Gulf and around Florida by water to St. Augustine. Far removed from the eyes of St. Augustine officials, this back-door route undoubtedly also was used to smuggle goods to and from ports in Cuba.

The importance of Apalachee is reflected in the rapid growth of missions in that province. In a few years nearly a dozen missions were built in major Apalachee towns, including in Ivitachuco (San Lorenzo de Ivitachuco), an important town on the eastern end of Apalachee territory.

Shortly after mid-century San Luis de Talimali, today located in Tallahassee, was founded. It would serve as the capital of Apalachee until the Apalachee missions were destroyed in the early eighteenth century. San

Luis, home to Spanish families who owned ranches in the province and were engaged in growing and exporting corn and other products, was the largest Spanish-Indian settlement outside St. Augustine. Apalachee was the colony's breadbasket, and colonial entrepreneurs, both Spaniards and Apalachee chiefs, were quick to exploit its productivity. San Luis prospered.

Initially each mission doctrina in Timucua and Apalachee served not only the Indians living in the mission village itself but the larger population who lived nearby in other villages or, in the case of Apalachee farmers, in farmsteads. In 1620, prior to the Apalachee missions, the 32 doctrinas of Guale and Timucua had 27 Franciscan priests serving more than 200 Indian villages.

As the seventeenth century wore on and Indian populations were steadily reduced by epidemics, these outlying villages disappeared. Remnant populations from the satellite towns were consolidated in each main mission village. By consolidating populations, the Spaniards were able to keep just under 40 doctrinas in Apalachee, Guale, and Timucua from the time of the founding of the Apalachee mission to at least 1675, even though the total Indian population of those areas declined greatly over that interval of time.

What were the missions like? The typical mission compound consisted of two buildings, with a third probably present at most: a church in which mass and other rites of the Catholic church could be performed by the friar; the friary or *convento*, where the friar lived; and, at some, a separate *cocina* or kitchen, where the friar's meals were prepared by Indian servants. The exact nature of these buildings differed across northern Florida, depending on when and where they were built.

Mission buildings typically fronted on the village plaza, which, at San Luis, also served as the field for the Apalachee stickball game. Portions of the mission compound were subdivided by fences, which also were used to enclose the gardens tended by villagers on behalf of the friars.

Some missions had large rectangular churches, measuring 60 by 35 feet; others were larger, as long as 100 feet. On one end were an exterior facade and an entryway; inside at the opposite end was a wood-floored sanctuary for the altar and for display of saints and other religious images. Off the sanctuary were one or two sacristies for storing vestments and other items. The largest part of the church interior was the nave, where Indian parishioners stood to attend mass. At some missions, the floor of the nave was packed clay, while at others it was earth. Rites, such as marriage ceremo-

◇ · ◇ · ◇ · ◇ · ◇ · ◇ · ◇ · ◇ · ◇ ·

## A Mission That Was; A Moat That Wasn't

In 1691, the governor of La Florida sent the king of Spain a drawing of Santa Catalina, built about 1686 on Amelia Island. It shows the mission buildings, plazas, a barracks, and a palisade and moat. The translated legend on the drawing reads:

> This palisade was constructed on the island of Santa María [Amelia Island] and place of Santa Catalina in the Province of Guale [actually it was in what had been Timucua territory]; the walls are three varas [1 vara is about 1 yard] high with bastions to fire arms; the bastions have earth ramps to half their height; there is a moat; and within it are the church, the convento of the doctrina, barracks for the infantry, and a small house for cooking.

The original of this drawing was found in the Spanish archives in Seville in the 1930s, and a copy was made for the University of Florida's P. K. Yonge Library of Florida History. I found it there in the mid-1980s when Rebecca Saunders, then one of my graduate students, and I were beginning to excavate the site of Santa Catalina on Amelia Island.

Listed in the card catalogue under "Missions—map," the drawing was easy to locate in the library. I was amazed that neither I nor another archaeologist had come across it earlier. And I was positively excited to locate a drawing of the exact mission we were investigating. In no time we began digging holes, looking for the moat and palisade.

Several times I was certain that I had found the moat; but Becky's subsequent meticulous excavations convinced me of the truth: there was no palisade and no moat. About that same time, historian Amy Turner Bushnell found post-1691 documents in which Spanish officials admitted that the palisade and moat had never been built. Their excuse? Not enough wood or labor. The governor had lied, and I had been embarrassed. Even so, this schematic representation of a church, convento, and cocina provides us with some idea of how mission buildings might ideally have been arranged and of their sizes relative to one another.

◇ · ◇ · ◇ · ◇ · ◇ · ◇ · ◇ · ◇ · ◇ ·

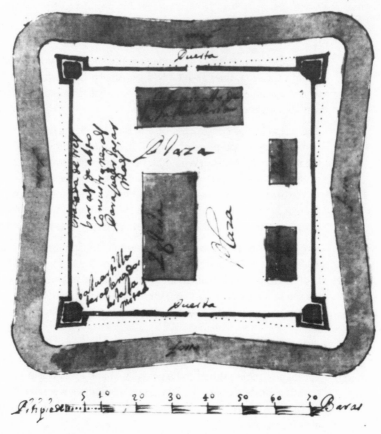

A 1691 drawing of Santa Catalina shows the moat that was not built. The church is the lower left building; across the plaza on its right are the convento (*lower*) and cocina (*upper*). The barracks for the contingent of Spanish soldiers stationed at the mission is north of the church across another plaza.

nies, were conducted near the door of the church. Just inside the door was a baptismal font carved from limestone or, perhaps, from wood.

Walls of churches were wattle and clay daub, which, when dried, could be plastered and painted. Roofs were thatched with palm or palmetto fronds. Conventos similarly were constructed of post and wattle-and-daub walls with thatched roofs. Churches were not mere huts. Their architectural refinements were intended to impress and to help convey the glory of Christianity.

A Florida Indian applies clay daub to a wattle framework attached to wall posts.

Some of the mission churches were less elaborate, having no walls at all. Instead they were open, pavilion-like structures with thatched roofs. And prior to a mission's construction of its church, mass might be conducted in a small chapel, little more than a covered sanctuary and sacristy. Worshippers stood in front of the chapel in the open. Such chapels probably were no longer used after the churches were built.

Construction of churches and conventos was done by native villagers using Spanish tools. Wrought-iron spikes and nails were employed, probably carried from St. Augustine. Because La Florida was a royal colony, funds and supplies, including tools for construction, were provided by the crown. As cumbersome as it may seem, such organization meant that Franciscans needing tools or supplies often wrote directly to the king. Such a request traveled by boat to Spain and then the answer returned on another ship. A simple request or complaint could take years to be handled. No wonder the friars took matters into their own hands and raised funds to pay for needed church supplies.

Christian Indians were afforded burial in the floor of the nave, or, in the case of chapels, around the exterior of the building. The numerous deaths of Christian Indians from diseases is reflected in the large number of interments made in churches, as many as 500 people in some. People were usually buried in individual shallow graves, lying on their backs with hands clasped or arms folded on chests. Bodies were placed in cloth shrouds pinned with brass straight pins. Some graves contain several individuals, probably reflecting epidemic deaths. Mission excavations by Bonnie McEwan and Clark Larsen at San Luis and by Rebecca Saunders at Santa Catalina on Amelia Island uncovered burials in wooden coffins, probably of native leaders. The Santa Catalina coffin, which contained two adult males, was crudely made with hewn logs and large iron spikes.

An integral part of each mission compound was a large brass bell suspended from a tower, at times a single post. The bell was literally the voice of the mission, summoning villagers and conveying information in times of danger. Bells were often named, a sign of their importance to a community.

Small contingents of Spanish soldiers, often less than a handful, were garrisoned at a few of the strategically placed missions in Timucua and Apalachee. They were quartered in their own housing but depended on villagers to provide food and to serve them. At San Luis there was a wooden fort with a moat and an interior strong house to offer protection to that important site and the Spanish families who lived there. The resident Spanish families maintained their houses in a section of the town fronting the plaza. Important Apalachee families probably also resided in the town but in a separate area from the Spaniards. Because of its Spanish residents and its status as the capital town of Apalachee, San Luis undoubtedly differed from other missions that had no Spanish residents other than friars and, on occasion, a few soldiers.

In those other mission towns the Indians, both chiefs and ordinary people, lived on the opposite side of the plaza from the mission buildings. Their houses were constructed of wood and thatch in the traditional manner, showing little Spanish influence.

Because missions were located in the main towns of each chiefdom, including in Apalachee, the native council house for each chiefdom was located on the same plaza as the mission buildings. The arrangement must have been an extraordinary sight. On the one side the church with its architectural finery, religious paintings and symbols, and Catholic santos and other iconography; on the other, as imposing in its own way, the large, circular Indian council house, likely displaying both native and Catholic iconography.

Council houses were the focus of native governmental activities, presided over by the village chief. As a part of those activities sacred teas were taken and other ceremonies were enacted. Visitors often were quartered in the council houses, and when Spanish officials met with native leaders, the meetings were conducted there. Within each council house was at least one circle of benches or semi-enclosed cabins—somewhat similar to box seats in a baseball stadium—lining the interior wall. Some of the larger council houses had a second circle of seats within that one. Interior support posts held up the radial rafters of the thatched roof, the central portion of which was left open. Directly under the opening was a large hearth where ceremonial fires were built, the smoke exiting through the roof opening. Around the fire within the circle of benches was a dance ground.

Seating within council houses was by a prescribed formula. The head chief sat in a certain place and his vassal chiefs in others. Other villagers were distributed according to their social and political status. Women generally did not participate in council house meetings, except in those Timucuan towns where women served as chiefs. But women did attend ceremonies taking place within the council house.

As befitted its status as the council house in the capital of Apalachee, San Luis's council house may have been the largest in all of Florida. Excavations by archaeologists of the Florida Bureau of Archaeological Research uncovered a building 120 feet in diameter with two concentric circles of benches and eight interior support posts. The roof opening over the fire was 46 feet across, while the dance ground was 65 feet in diameter. Visitors to San Luis can see this council house, which has been reconstructed at the state-owned site on Mission Road in Tallahassee. The churches and the Indian council houses are apt symbols of mission life, a blend of the new and the old.

Why did the Timucua and Apalachee Indians agree to become Christians? Franciscan friars and Spanish officials well understood the political systems of the Indians and the power of the chiefs. If chiefs could be convinced to become Catholics, their villagers would follow. The way the Spaniards persuaded chiefs to accept missionaries and to convert to Christianity was simple: bribery. Chiefs were invited to St. Augustine, where they were given presents—wheat flour, hoes, axes, blankets, and especially complete outfits of Spanish clothes. The Spanish were powerful allies who brought valued items and who, rather than usurping chiefly authority, reenforced it. Who could resist?

Lifeways that had served so well for generations were questioned when compared to the wonderful things brought by the Spaniards, including a new religion. As the influence of native priests lessened, that of Catholic friars grew. Once first generation conversions were made, the children who grew up as Catholics in the mission villages no longer knew many aspects of their traditional cultures. Heirs to chiefly positions were raised as members of the friar's entourage, assuring that when they became chiefs, they would be devout Catholics, loyal subjects of the Spanish crown, and devoted to the friars.

At the missions, villagers were taught religious doctrine and were given instruction in reading and writing in Spanish. They also received Christian names. Father Francisco Pareja at San Juan del Puerto wrote religious tracts and primers in the Timucua language using Spanish phonemes. According to Pareja, the books, distributed to other missions, were an effective way to teach Catholic discipline and doctrine. The pageantry, color, and essence of the Catholic religion replaced indigenous elements of native life. Mission Indians *were* Christians.

Missions also brought material changes. New plants grown in mission gardens and fields were added to the diet of the Apalachee and Timucua. Watermelons, wheat, peaches, figs, hazelnuts, oranges, and garbanzos have all have been identified from mission sites, while European greens, various herbs, peas, sugarcane, garlic, melons, barley, pomegranates, cucumbers, European grapes, cabbages, lettuce, and sweet potatoes are known to have been grown in St. Augustine and probably were cultivated at the missions as well.

Chickens and pigs were kept at the missions as, occasionally, were cattle and horses. Both Indian chiefs and Franciscan friars sold products from the missions to make money, a concept some Indians understood all too well. In 1695 two Apalachee Indians were arrested for counterfeiting Spanish coins!

In precolumbian times, villagers were required to provide labor to their chiefs for community projects, such as mound building at the Apalachee–Fort Walton town-centers. During the mission period, villagers continued to be required to perform labor for their chiefs but it was in support of the colony. Spanish officials issued orders listing the number of adult males that each mission was to furnish as laborers. These lists went to the village chiefs, who saw that the men were sent to St. Augustine, usually carrying corn or other goods from the missions on their backs. The Indians were supposed to be paid for their work, but the payments—trade goods—

## Piety of the Mission Indians

Did the Indians of northern Florida readily accept Christianity and its symbols? Or, as a few researchers have suggested, was Catholicism their public religion while in private they continued traditional beliefs? Certainly the Franciscan friars who had a vested interest in the success of the missions believed in the Christian piety of the Indians. In 1614 Father Francisco Pareja wrote:

> Among them are Indian men who have sufficient knowledge to give instructions while there are Indian women who catechize other Indian women, preparing them for the reception of Christianity. They assist at Masses of obligation on Sundays and feast-days in which they take part and sing; in some districts that have their confraternities and the precession of Holy Thursday, and from the mission stations they come to the principal mission to hear the *Salve* [the Salve Regina] which is sung on Saturdays. . . . They take holy water and recite their prayers in the morning and evening. They come together in the community house to teach one another singing and reading. . . . Do they confess as Christians? I answer yes. . . . Many persons are found, men and women, who confess and who receive [Holy Communion] with tears, and who show up advantageously with many Spaniards. And I shall make bold and say and sustain my contention by what I have learned by experience that with regard to the mysteries of the faith, many of them answer better than the Spaniards. (In Luís Gerónimo de Oré, *The Martyrs of Florida (1513–1616)*, Franciscan Studies 18 [New York: Joseph P. Wagner, 1936], 152–53)

Another friar noted:

> They respect the Holy Cross with such great love that they never step on its shadow, if they see it on the ground. Nor is it missing from their homes. And the first thing the heathens request of us when we arrive at their villages is that we raise it and hoist it on high. (In Hann, "1630 Memorial of Fray Francisco Alonso de Jesus," 101)

◇ · ◇ · ◇ · ◇ · ◇ · ◇ · ◇ · ◇ · ◇ ·

went to their chiefs. As a consequence, it was in the chiefs' best interests to support the labor quotas, and it was in the Spanish authorities' interests to support the chiefs.

Once in St. Augustine, Indians often were kept there for many months working. They tended fields that provided food for the garrison, worked on construction projects, timbered, and cut stone (coquina) in the mine on Anastasia Island. Indian laborers also performed tasks in Apalachee and Timucua for colonial authorities and for the friars. Trails had to be maintained by clearing brush, repairing creek crossings, and even building bridges. At river crossings too deep to ford, Indians were stationed to operate ferries; ferries also were operated between some of the islands on the northeast Florida coast.

Mission Indians served the friars and garrisoned soldiers, cooking, tending gardens, doing household chores, and hunting and gathering wild foods. Indian labor constructed buildings at the missions, including the San Luis fort, and Indian labor made possible the operation of Spanish-owned ranches in Timucua and Apalachee.

One of these ranches, on the north side of Paynes Prairie near present-day Gainesville, was La Chua, which by 1630 was a major producer of cattle and pigs. Two smaller ranches were also in what today is Alachua County, one on the south side of Paynes Prairie and one probably at San Felasco Hammock near the San Francisco mission. In western Timucua near the Aucilla River, there was a fourth ranch, a large one, which produced corn, wheat, and pigs.

Especially after the 1670s, Spanish settlers moved into Apalachee to operate ranches, and by 1698–99 there were nine ranches in that province. Most grew wheat and raised cattle, hogs, and horses. Prominent among the ranch owners were members of the Floréncia family, who lived at San Luis. A few ranch owners were Apalachee chiefs. Ranches worked by native laborers must have been money makers. Historian John Hann has documented more than two dozen ranches in eastern Florida, some of which were located east of the St. Johns River toward Cape Canaveral. At least one ranch was near or on the river in Mayaca territory.

That the lives of the Florida Indians changed dramatically during the colonial period is abundantly clear. In 1513 they had never seen a horse or a cow. A century and a half later they were raising these animals. It is no exaggeration to say that La Florida rested on the shoulders and backs of Florida Indians. As the number of native people at the Timucua missions west of the St. Johns River continued to drop due to diseases, Spanish officials adopted several strategies to keep the mission villages populated so that the colony could be assured of sufficient labor. One strategy was to consolidate the villages served by a mission—as noted, people from satellite villages were resettled at the main villages. Another ploy was to move people from areas with larger populations to the missions that needed people. The problem was not as acute in Apalachee, which, when missions were first established there, had a larger population. Also, the first missions in Apalachee were established a quarter-century after the first Potano and Timucua missions in north Florida. The ravages of the early (pre-1633) epidemics may not have reached the Apalachee.

In 1656, a rebellion occurred, offering the governor of Spanish Florida the excuse to reorganize the Timucuan missions totally as a way to cope with their dwindling population. That such a reorganization occurred was unknown until a few years ago, when archival evidence was found by anthropologist John Worth.

The rebellion was an attempt by some of the Timucuan chiefs to free themselves from Spanish labor demands and to retaliate for the perceived lack of respect paid them by the governor, Diego de Rebolledo. It soon ended with minimal loss of Spanish life. But faced with inadequate labor to maintain trails, operate ferries across rivers, and provide other services, the governor turned punishment of the rebellious Timucua to Spanish advantage. He ordered abandonment of some missions and relocation of others; new missions were founded. The result was that nearly all the surviving Timucua Indians were living in missions approximately a day's travel apart on a single trail, the trail known as the *camino real,* the royal road, the main east-west trail from St. Augustine across Timucua to Apalachee.

For the remainder of the seventeenth century, the Timucua missions were way stations along the camino real, the most direct route from St. Augustine to the ranches in Apalachee. Timucuan villagers maintained the road and manned ferries on the Suwannee River.

The population of the Timucua continued to drop, while that of Apalachee appears to have stabilized at about 8,500 people. Faced with a potential collapse of the mission system in north peninsular Florida, Spanish officials and Franciscan friars looked farther south in Florida for new converts, Indians who could be brought to Christianity, taught agricultural methods, and perhaps moved to north Florida. But attempts in the 1690s to establish new missions among the Calusa Indians in southwest Florida and the Jororo and perhaps the Ais in central Florida failed.

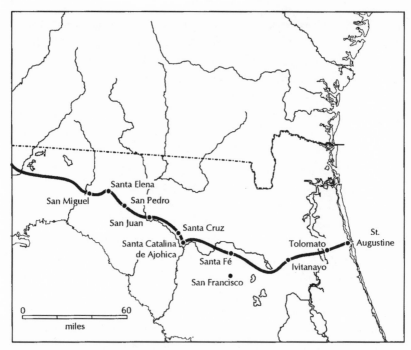

The Timucuan missions positioned along the camino real following the 1656 rebellion

Indians from Georgia and even South Carolina were moved into Florida to repopulate missions. All efforts would be in vain, however. The eighteenth century would see the destruction of the Apalachee and Timucuan missions and the decimation of the Florida Indians. Caught up in the conflict between Great Britain and Spain, the Indians of northern Florida would be gone by 1710, leaving the rest of Florida open to raids by native slavers. In another 50 years, the human legacy of more than ten millennia would disappear.

# 10  An End and a New Beginning

Bubonic plague, chicken pox, dysentery, diphtheria, influenza, malaria, measles, scarlet fever, smallpox, typhoid, typhus, yellow fever. To this list add secondary infections like pneumonia, ill health caused by mistreatment and forced labor, and raids by Indian and Carolinian slavers and militia. These were the scourges that decimated the Timucua and reduced the Apalachee Indians from as many as 50,000 people to 8,500 people by 1700.

Epidemics that hit the missions of northern Florida in 1595, 1612–1617, 1649–50, and 1655–56 most likely also killed nonmission Indians living elsewhere in Florida. Microbes did not discriminate between Christian and non-Christians; colonization was not kind to any of Florida's Indians.

Great Britain, Spain's rival for the eastern seaboard, recognized the importance of the missions to the colony of La Florida. Weakening the missions would weaken Spain's hold on La Florida. Having established the Charlestowne settlement in 1670—modern Charleston in South Carolina—British interests began to chip away at the missions, beginning with raids in 1680 on San Buenaventura de Guadalquini on St. Simons Island and Santa Catalina de Guale, both on the Georgia coast. In each case the Indian raiding party was abetted by Carolinian or English soldiers.

More attacks on the coastal missions followed in 1684. These raids made it clear to Spanish authorities that they did not have the resources to defend the coastal missions. Early the next year, all the Guale and Timucuan missions on the Georgia coast were withdrawn. Spain had retreated in the face of Carolinian aggressions. As a result, the northernmost missions were on Amelia Island only 50 miles north of St. Augustine.

Some villagers from the raided missions fled the coast, while others, including Yamasee Indians who had moved to the Guale missions from South Carolina and Georgia, gave up their Spanish affiliation and moved back northward to live as allies of the Carolinians. But not all went voluntarily; some were taken as slaves. The Spaniards relocated other villagers to missions on Amelia Island and farther south. In one case Yamasee people were resettled far to the south at a mission among the Mayaca Indians that was in need of villagers.

Having accomplished their objectives on the Georgia coast, the Carolinians began to hammer at the fragile interior Timucuan missions on the camino real, hoping to sever the transportation link between Apalachee's productive fields and St. Augustine. In a 1685 raid on Santa Catalina de Afuica, a new mission founded on the camino real in southeast Suwannee County after the 1656 rebellion, native slavers carried back Timucua Indians to be sold in South Carolina. Six years later slavers hit San Juan de Guacara in western Suwannee County. Raids also struck at isolated missions north and west of the Apalachee province in the Flint and Apalachicola river drainages. Presumably the fort built earlier at San Luis afforded protection to the Apalachee missions proper.

Two additional Timucua missions—San Pedro y San Pablo de Potohiriba and Santa Fe—were attacked in 1702 by Apalachicola Indians aided by Carolinians. Spanish soldiers stationed at Santa Fe successfully defended the mission but then walked into an ambush when they attempted a counterattack, an ill thought-out action resulting in Timucua and Spanish deaths.

Late in 1702, Carolinian militiamen and native allies, including some Yamasee Indians, sailed from Port Royal near Charleston to attack St. Augustine. Commanded by Governor James Moore, the army first landed on the northern end of Amelia Island, quickly taking the Spanish garrison stationed near modern Fernandina Beach. Marching down the island, the army wiped out Santa Clara de Tupique and San Felipe before reaching Santa Catalina, the Guale mission resettled on Amelia Island from Georgia only six years earlier. Warned of the impending attack, the Spanish soldiers, friars, and villagers at Santa Catalina fled. The mission, next to Harrison Creek, was set ablaze; its remains were found and excavated by archaeologists in the 1980s.

Continuing south, the raiders crossed to Fort George Island and destroyed San Juan de Puerto. First founded 115 years earlier, in 1587, San Juan was the last Spanish outpost between the Carolinians and St. Augustine. The army marched on the town and laid siege to the stone fort where the residents of St. Augustine had fled for protection.

Unable to breach the coquina walls of the fort after several weeks, the Carolinian army lifted the siege and then withdrew, but not before burning the town and capturing 500 Indians who were taken to be sold into slavery. St. Augustine survived, but the chain of missions to the north was gone and the Indian mission residents were either captives or refugees or they had switched their allegiance to the Carolinians in order to avoid enslavement.

Apalachee and Timucua would fall next. Three missions were destroyed in 1703 in a raid by Carolinian militia and Indians. The next year two large, well-organized raids, again led by Moore, swept through Apalachee, devastating missions. Churches were sacked and burned, mission bells were hammered into submission, Catholic Indians were tortured. Three hundred men and a thousand women and children were forcibly taken back to South Carolina and resettled there. Several thousand Indians were taken to be sold to plantations. Other mission Indians opted simply to desert the missions and follow the raiders back to the Carolinas. Spanish residents in Apalachee province also fled, some to Pensacola, where a fort had been built in 1698. Smaller raids in 1705–7 finished off the missions, in the process routing Spanish soldiers recently stationed in the provinces to protect them.

The landscape of Leon and Jefferson counties was littered with the burned remains of the Apalachee missions. Ranches were abandoned. Timucuan missions also had been burned and that province devastated. Having numbered about 9,000 in 1700, the Indians of the Apalachee and Timucuan missions had now been killed or taken captive, had fled northern Florida, or were living in refugee villages near St. Augustine. Among the Apalachee who had escaped to the west were the ancestors of the Apalachee Indians who today live in Louisiana.

In 1710 northern Florida was said to be a ghost land. The refugee villages around St. Augustine, still served by Franciscan friars, had few inhabitants. A census taken in 1717 lists only 942 Indians living in ten towns.

◇ · ◇ · ◇ · ◇ · ◇ · ◇ · ◇ · ◇ · ◇ ·

## The Raids of 1702, 1703, and Early 1704

In March 1704, the governor of La Florida, Don Joseph de Zúñiga y
Zerda, sent the king a report from St. Augustine recounting the results
of the raids that had taken place after the besieging of that settlement
in 1702:

> In the incursions they have made since the siege, San Joseph de
> Ocuia in Apalachee, Pilitiriva [San Pedro y San Pablo de Potohir-
> iba in Timucua], and San Francisco [de Potano] have all been de-
> stroyed and many Indians killed, and in all they have carried off
> more than five hundred prisoners. . . . They have now returned
> to Apalachee, accompanied by the governor [James Moore] who
> here besieged me, with a force of fifteen hundred Indians and
> fifty English, desolating the country, and assaulting the place of
> [La Concepción de] Ayubale [in Apalachee] on the 25th of Janu-
> ary of this year, which was defended with all bravery by the Indi-
> ans and the parish priest Fray Angel de Miranda, who fought
> from morning until two in the afternoon, when their munitions
> gave out. The enemy advanced to the stockade close by the
> church and convent, which they set fire and captured. On the
> 26th my deputy in Apalachee, Captain Juan Ruíz de Mexía, with
> about thirty Spanish soldiers and settlers, and four hundred Apa-
> lachee Indians, surrounded the enemy and killed six or seven of
> the English and about one hundred of the pagan Indians, to say
> nothing of another fifty killed by the priest Miranda and the Indi-
> ans of Ayubale, and two or three English more. But finally, for
> lack of munitions, my people were defeated, (and) my deputy
> was wounded by a ball which toppled him from his horse. They
> also killed the parish priest of [San Pedro y San Pablo de] Patale
> [in Apalachee], who wished to accompany them, and two soldiers
> and some Indians who were roasted with much barbarity and cru-
> elty by the abhorrent pagans, who bound them to some stakes
> by the feet and hands and set them afire until their lives were ex-
> tinguished. . . . The enemy freed my deputy, the priest Miranda,
> and four of the soldiers, on the supposition that they could exact
> a ransom of four hundred pesos in reals, with five cows and five
> horses for each. . . . On their withdrawal, they left five [missions]
> destroyed, and of these, the entire population of two (places) ac-
> companied them voluntarily. They carried off all that could not
> be collected, including cows and horses. . . . The enemy carried
> off more than six hundred of the Christian Indians. (Mark F. Boyd,
> Hale G. Smith, and John W. Griffin, *Here They Once Stood*
> [Gainesville: University of Florida Press, 1951], 48–50)

◇ · ◇ · ◇ · ◇ · ◇ · ◇ · ◇ · ◇ · ◇ ·

They included Apalachee, Guale, Mayaca, Timucua, and Yamasee Indians, remnants from the Florida and Georgia missions.

The Carolinian attacks that had devastated the missions opened peninsular Florida to further raids by native slavers. With no Spanish presence in the northern part of the state to halt them, Lower Creek, Westo, and Savannah Indians, as well as Yamasee Indians friendly to the Carolinians, sought captives to be sold in Charleston. The peoples of central and southern Florida, like the Jororo and the Calusa, were now fair game for raids by Indians armed with guns obtained from English-backed traders.

Some of these Florida Indians fled south to try to avoid the raiders. Others—including Tocobaga, Jororo, and Pohoy Indians—sought protection in the refugee villages around St. Augustine. As a result, by 1726 the number of villages had increased to 12, with a total population of slightly more than 1,000. But the presence of St. Augustine's stone castillo did little to deflect additional raiders, who saw the refugee towns as easy targets. Yuchi and Tallapoosa Indians raided villages almost in the shadow of the castillo walls. In 1727 an epidemic hit the refugee towns, further decimating them.

The next year saw an attack by 200 Carolinian militia and Indians on Nombre de Dios, just north of St. Augustine's city gates. A decade later only eight refugee villages with a population of 340 remained. The villages continued to fade away as disease claimed lives and remnant populations were consolidated.

As late as 1759 two mission towns, Tolomato and Nombre de Dios, also known as Nuestra Señora de la Leche, were occupied and served by friars. Their combined population was only 95 people. Four years later Spain and Great Britain signed a treaty ending hostilities between them. St. Augustine was ceded to the British in exchange for Havana, which earlier had been captured by British soldiers. In 1763 and 1764 the Spaniards withdrew from St. Augustine and their La Florida colony. The 89 Indians living in St. Augustine and at Tolomato and Nuestra Señora de la Leche were taken to Cuba with the Spaniards, then sent to the town of Guanabacoa.

Florida Indians who had elected to move southward down the peninsula to escape the slave raids did not find sanctuary. Even at the very tip of the state they were not safe. The bishop of Cuba, writing in 1711, summarized the situation:

In the past month . . . a ship entered this port, which had come from the keys. . . . The heathen Indians of the chiefs, Carlos, Coleto, and others live in those keys. And some of the above-mentioned Indians who came in the aforesaid ship told me about very serious persecutions and hostilities, which they are experiencing and which they have experienced on other keys, which the Indians whom they call Yamasees have destroyed. That the Yamasees have killed some of the aforementioned Keys Indians; have made others flee; and that they have captured the greater part of the latter, whom, it is said, they carry off and sell, placing them into slavery at the port of [Charleston]. (Hann, *Missions to the Calusa*, p. 46)

Small groups of Indians continued to live in southern Florida. In 1743, 180 people were living in a village at the mouth of the Miami River, where the Tequesta Indians had once lived. The group included Keys, Calusa, and Boca Raton Indians. Two Jesuit priests accompanied by Spanish soldiers were sent to the village to minister to the Indians. But the mission they established, Santa María de Loreto, was only short-lived. While the Jesuits were in the Miami area, they noted that three other enclaves of refugee Indians—Mayaimies, Santaluces, and Mayacas—were said to be living one, two, and four days' travel from Santa María. Together the three groups included just over 100 people. Presumably they were living in the interior of southern Florida and not in the Florida Keys.

The Indians living in the Miami area and in the Florida Keys in the eighteenth century were not isolated from colonial endeavors. Hispanic fishermen from both Cuba and St. Augustine used the Indians as laborers on fishing boats and at fishing ranchos on the Florida coasts, where fish were dried, packed, and shipped. The Florida Indians were willing to take such work because it allowed them access to the trade items on which they had come to depend. At least some of the Indians sailed to Cuba with the fleets; others intermarried with the fishermen. These Spanish Indians, as they were known, probably lived a life combining aspects of indigenous and Hispanic cultures. We might guess that they spoke Spanish as well as native languages and that marriages resulted in a growing mestizo population equally at home in St. Augustine or a Cuban port as at a coastal fishing rancho occupied mainly by Indians.

The fishing industry would continue even after the Spaniards withdrew from Florida with labor provided by Seminole Indians. By the first few decades of the nineteenth century, fishing ranchos were found from Jupiter Inlet south to the Florida Keys and up the Gulf coast to Tampa Bay. There is still much to learn about this fishing industry and the interactions among the Native American, Hispanic, and mestizo workers.

In the mid-eighteenth century at the time of mission Santa Maria de Loreto and while the fishing industry was in operation, it is likely that refugee Indians other than those we know about were living in Florida. But for all practical purposes, the native people of Florida were gone, their ethnic identities shattered.

The population vacuum attracted not only Indians who saw opportunities in raiding the few refugees in central and southern Florida. It also drew Indians who sought a different kind of wealth: land and the desire to live in peace, free from the international and intertribal conflicts being played out just to the north of Florida. Most of these latter Indians were Lower Creeks from Georgia and Alabama who sought independence from the Upper Creeks. The Creek confederacy had formed by about 1700 and included native people who were the descendants of the once numerous Mississippian cultures that had dominated the interior Southeast during the late precolumbian period.

Florida contained fertile lands for agriculture and for raising livestock. Locales that once had sustained Spanish and Indian missions and ranches in northwest and north Florida became home to Creek Indians. Two areas were especially important in this period of early migration into Florida, the Tallahassee–Lake Miccosukee area in what had been Apalachee province and the Gainesville–Paynes Prairie region in Timucua. A few early Creek towns were west of Apalachee in the Apalachicola River drainage, while still others were west of Gainesville near the lower Suwannee River.

Spanish officials actively encouraged this initial movement of Creeks into Florida. With the demise of the missions, St. Augustine sorely needed native allies. In Florida, the Creeks were quick to establish avenues of trade and they were not shy about playing off the Spaniards against Spain's colonial rival, Great Britain and her colonies. Florida presented new opportunities and the Indians took advantage of them.

Artifacts recovered from archaeological sites associated with these early towns indicate that the Florida Creeks initially lived much like their Creek relatives to the north. But gradually they became independent of the more northerly Creeks and developed a way of life suited to their new surroundings. They also received a new name. By the 1760s these Florida Indians were becoming known as the Seminoles.

Each Seminole town maintained its own identity and name. In the 1770s naturalist William Bartram visited three of them: Cuscowilla near Paynes Prairie south of Gainesville, Talahoschte on the Suwannee River to the west of Gainesville, and a town on the St. Johns River near Palatka. Both

Cuscowilla and Talahoschte consisted of about 30 households with gardens in which corn, beans, squash, melons, oranges, and tobacco were cultivated. At Cuscowilla agricultural fields were a distance away from the town center, where a Creek-style squareground was located. Individual households were scattered, rather than being located around the central squareground. Talahoschte, with a more compact town arrangement, had a similar squareground, described as three "cabins" or covered seating areas arranged around a central plaza. There the business of the town was conducted, as were certain ceremonies.

The squareground of the Seminole town near Palatka was smaller and featured a pavilion-like structure as its council area. Bartram described it as

> a grand, airy pavilion in the center of the village. It was four square; a range of pillars and posts on each side supporting a canopy composed of Palmetto leaves, woven or thatched together, which shaded a level platform in the center, that was ascended from each side by two steps or flights, each almost twelve inches high, and seven or eight feet in breadth, all covered with carpets, curiously woven, of split canes dyed of various colors. (William Bartram, *The Travels of William Bartram*, ed. Mark van Doren [New York: Dover, 1955], pp. 250–51)

Such covered squaregrounds, which bear resemblances to the later open thatched chickees of the Seminoles in southern Florida, apparently were traditional among Creek Indians in earlier times. The more open squaregrounds of Cuscowilla and Talahoschte were a later adaptation.

Important aspects of Creek life were retained by the Seminoles, including the stickball game and ceremonies like the smoking of the calumet or peace pipe, taking of black drink, and celebration of the busk or Green Corn dance with its rituals revolving around purity, agricultural fertility, and maintaining the balance of the world. This is not surprising, because these activities and beliefs have a long history among the native peoples of the Southeast, including the ancestors of the Seminoles.

Like other southeastern native societies, the Seminoles were matrilineal: children belonged to the same clan as their mothers. When a young man married it was to a woman outside his own clan, and he moved to the household of his bride. There he lived among women who might span three or more generations, all of the same clan. A single household might consist of a great-grandmother, a grandmother, her daughters, and the adult daughters' unmarried children and married daughters. Clans would become important economic units within Seminole culture, both for the production of food and goods and for trade.

Seminole Indians were actively involved in bartering with white traders, exchanging honey, cow and deer hides, garden produce, and other commodities for European ceramics and containers, tomahawks, razors, knives, metal buttons, guns and gun parts, gunpowder and ammunition, mirrors, horse tack, glass beads, and many other items. Women were full participants in this trade, exchanging the products of their gardening efforts for goods.

The Cuscowilla Seminole Indians, led by the famous chief Cowkeeper, also kept cattle, herds apparently descended from those of the abandoned Spanish ranches around Paynes Prairie. Some anthropologists have suggested that the more dispersed community plan of the Cuscowilla Seminole town may have been a result of the importance of cattle ownership by individuals. Herds needed much more land than did gardens and agricultural fields.

The opportunities to acquire wealth through shrewd trading and individual initiative made entrepreneurs out of many Seminoles. Men and women acquired status and power from accomplishments, not merely inheriting social position. Individual families grew economically important as village ties loosened. New towns were founded by leaders who achieved success through personal accomplishments. Individuals and their families, not town councils and hereditary leaders, began to emerge as economic decision makers. A distinctive Seminole way of life different from that of the Creek Indians was evolving.

Other Indians in addition to Lower Creeks also migrated to Florida during this early period; some may originally have been raiders from the north who stayed. Among them were Yuchi and Yamasee Indians. Black slaves who had escaped from plantations in the Carolinas and Georgia moved into Florida, at times living near Seminole towns in separate communities. Both black people and non-Seminole Indians also were kept as slaves, while other individuals were integrated into Seminole society. Refugees from the Spanish missions still living in Florida may also have joined the Seminoles. William Bartram observed one such Spanish-speaking Indian wearing a cross and living at Cuscowilla.

In the early nineteenth century another large migration of Creeks took place. Perhaps a thousand Upper Creeks moved to Florida following Andrew Jackson's 1814 defeat of Upper Creek warriors at the Battle of Tohopeka. For Jackson, interceding in what had essentially been a Creek civil war had been a way to deal a blow to the Indian population and free lands for settlers from the expanding United States. He sided with one group of Upper Creeks against the Upper Creek faction known as "Red Sticks," named for their red war clubs. It was the latter who migrated into Florida.

Jackson's ploy was successful. The Treaty of Fort Jackson in 1815, signed by Creek chiefs loyal to the United States, took 22 million acres of what had been Creek land in Georgia and Alabama for the United States. The Creeks who had remained loyal to the United States were given land in southeast Alabama, though that land was to be held in trust by the government. Through the 1830s and 1840s, the time of Indian removal, some of these Creeks and their descendants were allowed to remain in Alabama. Others moved into the Florida panhandle or lived in Alabama apart from Creek communities, gradually becoming assimilated into white society.

The Alabama Creeks who were not forced to move west were the ancestors of the federally recognized Poarch Creeks, whose headquarters are in Atmore, Alabama, but who live in both Florida and Alabama. Descendants of other Creek Indians, some associated with the Florida Tribe of Eastern Creeks, live mainly in Walton and Calhoun counties, while the Muscogee Creek Indian Tribe is centered in Taylor County. A contingent of Creek Indians also lives in Escambia County.

By 1820, after the influx of Creek Indians following what had been called the Red Stick War, there were 5,000 Creek and Seminole Indians living in Florida. New Seminole towns were established from south of Gainesville down to Tampa Bay.

In 1819 Florida had been made a territory of the United States. American settlers from Georgia and the Carolinas soon began to pour into the state to farm the same lands that had drawn Creek Indians in the eighteenth century. Conflicts between Seminoles and settlers were inevitable. Even before Spain, which had regained control of Florida from Britain in 1783 following the American Revolutionary War, relinquished La Florida to the United States, Andrew Jackson had used such conflicts as an excuse to wage war against the Seminole Indians. In 1817, Jackson had invaded Spanish Florida and attacked Seminole towns, pushing some bands down the peninsula. It was two years after that engagement, the First Seminole War, that Spain ceded Florida to the United States.

But even after Jackson's raids, many Seminoles still remained in northern Florida, the new southern frontier of the expanding United States. Disputes arose over runaway slaves and other issues. In 1823, in an effort to prevent further friction between settlers and Seminoles, the United States signed the Treaty of Moultrie Creek with several Seminole chiefs. The treaty forced the Seminoles to agree to move to lands in the central part of the state, from Fort King—near modern Ocala—south to Lake Okeechobee. For the most part this region was south of the old mission provinces of Apalachee and Timucua. Seminole towns shifted southward into central Florida, including around the many lakes in the Orlando–Winter Park area.

In 1830, during the administration of Andrew Jackson, newly elected U.S. president, the Indian Removal Act became the law of the land. The southeastern Indians were to be moved west of the Mississippi River to Indian Territory, today the state of Oklahoma. The Seminoles simply refused to go, although a delegation was sent to inspect the lands intended for their use in Oklahoma. While there, Seminole members of the delegation signed a treaty agreeing to removal. But, claiming they had been duped, the signers disavowed the treaty once they returned to Florida. Federal militia were sent to deal with the situation; armed conflict was inevitable.

Led by Osceola, Seminole warriors raided an army supply train south of Gainesville in 1835; ten days later other Seminoles attacked and decimated a contingent of more than 100 soldiers, the infamous Dade Massacre in Sumter County. The Second Seminole War was under way.

Two years later almost to the day, 400 Seminole warriors and 800 federal troops fought a pitched battle just north of Lake Okeechobee. From that engagement the Seminole learned not to face federal troops in an open test of firepower. Instead, the Seminoles would opt to fight a guerilla war with raids and skirmishes. But even so, many Seminoles were captured or surrendered. Once in federal custody they were shipped to Indian Territory. By 1842 when the war was declared over, only 200–300 Seminoles remained in Florida of the 6,000 who had once lived there. Small bands sought refuge in the isolated Everglades and swamps of the south.

In only a few short years, the relentless southward push of the frontier would again catch up with the Seminole. In 1855, ten years after Florida had become a state, Seminole Indians and military surveyors exchanged shots. The Third Seminole War, sometimes called the Billy Bowlegs War, had begun, amid new demands to remove the remaining Seminoles to Indian Territory.

The war, a series of limited engagements, was fought in southern Florida. It drew to a close in 1858 only after troops were able to penetrate the

A Seminole Indian chickee in south Florida in the 1880s. Clay MacCauley wrote of seeing a rifle with powder horn and shot flask, a hoe, a log mortar two feet high, with pestle, and a bag of corn hanging from the house rafters. To the right of the house in the sawgrass is a dugout canoe.

Big Cypress Swamp and destroy Seminole settlements and stored food supplies. About 150 Seminoles were shipped to Oklahoma, again leaving only a few hundred Indians scattered among the Everglades, the Big Cypress Swamp, and the Ten Thousand Islands. It is the descendants of those unconquered Seminoles who today live in Florida.

Following the Third Seminole War, the Seminole Indians lived in relative isolation in south Florida for several decades. They made their livelihood by hunting, fishing, and collecting wild foods as well as cultivating gardens with a variety of fruits and vegetables and keeping chickens and some livestock. Small settlements, each with several chickees, dotted the hammocks and other high ground around Lake Okeechobee and in the Everglades and Big Cypress Swamp to the south. Interior southern Florida was the land of the Seminoles, who plied its hidden waterways in cypress canoes.

Toward the end of the nineteenth century, trading posts were established at Ft. Lauderdale, Chokoloskee, and other locations. Seminoles traded alligator hides and egret feathers, valued items in the world of American fashion far from south Florida, for sewing machines and other goods. The life they made for themselves in the south Florida wetlands was far different from that of the precolumbian inhabitants of the same region.

The massive drainage projects that began in southern Florida in the

A Seminole chickee near the Tamiami Trail in the 1950s

Seminole Indians in canoes on the Miami River, probably in the late 1880s or early 1890s. This photograph is thought to have been taken near the trading post run by the Brickell family on the south side of the river near its mouth.

A Seminole man poles a dugout canoe through the Everglades, ca. 1951

Ingraham Billie, a Mikasuki medicine man, with his family in front of this camp and souvenir store on the Tamiami Trail, 1938

Herding cattle on the Brighton Reservation, 1950s

1890s would help to dry up the Seminoles' new economic pursuits. Then came the early twentieth-century boom that brought new residents to south Florida. Miami, Fort Lauderdale, and Fort Myers soon were on their way to being the cities they are today. The Seminoles began to stress tourism as one way to earn money to subsist. In the 1930s and 1940s, some of the Seminoles began to herd cattle, returning to a resource that their ancestors had turned to a century before.

During this time federal agencies provided some services for the Seminole people, but these were threatened in the 1950s by federal legislation that sought to remove the special status of American Indian tribes. That possibility prompted the Seminoles to organize in a more formal fashion, and on August 21, 1957, the Seminoles voted to become the Seminole Tribe of Florida.

Most people do not realize that among the Seminole Indians, two different Creek languages have been spoken since their forebears first entered Florida. One language is Muskogee, sometimes called Creek, and the other Mikasuki, sometimes called Hitchiti. Both are Muskogean languages, belonging to the same family of languages present across much of the precolumbian Southeast.

◇ · ◇ · ◇ · ◇ · ◇ · ◇ · ◇ · ◇ · ◇

## Seminole Indian Enterprise

Living as an American Indian is not easy. The unemployment rate on south Florida's Miccosukee and Seminole reservations and trust lands is about 35 percent; for Indians living off the reservations or in urban areas it is between 25 and 30 percent. Dismal as these figures may seem, they do represent an improvement over the recent past, thanks to efforts by the Indians themselves.

Florida tribes have initiated various entrepreneurial endeavors to provide more economic opportunities for their people. One business is high-stakes bingo, a controversial undertaking that has drawn criticism from some quarters. But bingo and other businesses are helping Florida's Indians to begin to share more fully in the state's prosperity and to strive toward receiving the same level of services afforded other citizens. As explained in the World Wide Web home page of the Seminole Tribe of Florida:

> Gaming income funds the administration of the tribal government, tribal parks and recreational facilities and services, tribal member services, education programs and economic development on the reservations that otherwise would not exist. Tribal gaming is a government-sponsored activity whose proceeds are used exclusively for the benefit of The Seminole Tribe. Gaming has allowed the Tribe to meet its own needs, rather than relying on handouts from the federal government.

> The economic impact of Seminole gaming reaches far beyond the reservations, and contributes significantly to the economy of the State of Florida. Seminole gaming establishments employ 2,200 Floridians, 95 percent of whom are non-Indian. With a payroll of almost $25 million, Seminole gaming activities generate more than $3.5 million a year in payroll taxes and unemployment insurance payments. Seminole gaming establishments purchase more that $24 million in goods and services from more than 850 Florida vendors each year, as well. These dollars go to education, health care, infrastructure development, fire and emergency management services, economic development activities and delivery of other basic government services to tribal members. (http://www.seminoletribe.com/enterprises/gaming.shtm)

Self-reliance and successful adjustments to changing conditions are hallmarks of Florida's Indians.

◇ · ◇ · ◇ · ◇ · ◇ · ◇ · ◇ · ◇ · ◇

Not only are there two different languages spoken among the south Florida Indians; there are two political entities as well. Floridians were amazed in 1962 when the Miccosukee Tribe was formally recognized by the federal government. Few people realized that the Miccosukee had long been in Florida; most people simply thought they were Seminoles.

◇　·　◇　·　◇　·　◇　·　◇　·　◇　·　◇　·　◇　·　◇　·

### Seminole Florida

A great many modern Florida place-names are derived from the Mikasuki and Muskogee languages and from the people who speak them. In a few cases, names are Indian pronunciations of Spanish names. For instance, the Suwannee River is derived from a Seminole enunciation of the mission of San Juan—pronounced "San Juan-ee"—located near Charles Spring in western Suwannee County. Mission San Francisco became San Felasco, the modern name of the dry prairie just north of the mission site. In the latter case, the "r" sound became an "l" sound, accompanied by a consonant shift. Similar shifts took place in the pronunciation of the Spanish word *cimarrones*, to become Seminoles. Cimarrones, meaning "runaways," was a term used to refer to Creek Indians who had chosen to leave their traditional lands and resettle in Florida. The Muskogee and Mikasuki languages provide important links to Florida's past.

Many more Mikasuki and Muskogee words identify the landscape, some mispronounced by non-Indian tongues. Here are just a few: Allapattah, Apopka, Bithlo, Chassahowitzka, Chattahoochee, Chokolaskee, Chuluota, Econfina, Efaw, Fenholloway, Istachata, Loxahatchee, Narcoosee, Okeechobee, Ocklawaha, Panasoffkee, Tsala-Apopa, Wacahoota, Wekiwachee, Wekiwa, and Wewahitchka. In general, Florida place-names ending in -sassa,-hatchee, and-ee are Seminole in origin.

A third group of place-names are English translations of harder-to-pronounce Indian names. Two of my favorites are Wewahaiyayaki, "shining water," which in English is Crystal River, and Thlathlo-popka-hachi, "fish-eating river," which is Fisheating Creek.

We also are indebted to Seminole peoples for the names of Seminole and Osceola counties, the small towns of Aripeka and Emathla, and Paynes Prairie, which takes its name from the famed Seminole leader Chief Payne. Even the name of Florida's capital, Tallahassee, once a Seminole town, is testimony to the state's Native American heritage.

◇　·　◇　·　◇　·　◇　·　◇　·　◇　·　◇　·　◇　·　◇　·

The Miccosukee Indians are descendants of a Lower Creek group, the Mikasuki, who had migrated to Florida as much as two centuries earlier. The history of Seminole peoples in Florida is really the history of Seminole and Miccosukee peoples. Today Florida has three federally recognized Native American tribes: the Seminole, the Miccosukee, and the Poarch Creeks.

As extraordinary as it may seem, these three tribes are a minority within the Native American population of modern Florida. In the U.S. 1990 census, 36,335 people (out of 13 million total Florida residents) identified themselves as American Indians. Of that number, less than a tenth are Seminole, Miccosukee, and Poarch Creeks. Who are the other more than 30,000 Indians living in Florida? They include people from 48 different tribes, groups such as the Lumbee, Choctaw, Chippewa, and other Creeks. According to the census, there are more Cherokee Indians in Florida than members of any other tribe; 10,000 people cite Cherokee affiliation.

How accurate is the 36,335 figure? No one knows for certain. Demographers and even some Florida Indians suspect that many individuals who claim to be Native Americans may actually be people who like to identify with Indians. On the other hand, during the twentieth century, the number of Indians living in Florida has steadily increased, from 358 in 1900 to 1,011 in 1950. By 1970 that number had grown to 6,617, perhaps reflecting the moving to Florida of Indians who sought the same things other Americans were seeking: a good climate and economic opportunities.

From 1970 to the present, the growth of Florida's Native American population has been phenomenal: from 6,671 in 1970 to 19,316 in 1980 to 36,335 in 1990. The U.S. Census Bureau predicts that in the year 2000, Florida's 15.2 million residents will include 51,000 American Indians. Such population growth would seem to be unprecedented. On the other hand, those 36,335 individuals identified in the 1990 census constitute only 0.28 percent of the total Florida population. Just who should be considered a "real" Indian and who should not will continue to be a debatable point among Native Americans and demographers alike.

What is important is that Florida is home to a substantial number of people of American Indian descent. As we enter a new millennium, Florida's Indians will have a significant role in helping all of us to understand the past and to plan for our shared future.

# For Further Reading and Research

## Resources On-Line

The Florida Bureau of Archaeological Research, a branch of the Department of State's Division of Historical Resources, maintains a comprehensive and frequently updated web page that contains information on Florida's Indians and archaeology, including materials for children and links to a host of other pertinent Internet addresses. The latter include museum exhibits and archaeological and historical sites that can be visited. The bureau's Internet address is www.dos.state.fl.us/dhr/bar.

Another informative web page is maintained by the Seminole Tribe of Florida. Through the page one can find information on the history of the Seminole people and learn about their lives today. Links also are provided to the Seminole Indian Museum in south Florida and to activities open to the public. The address is www.seminoletribe.com.

## The Written Word

Listed here are just a few of the many books that have been written about Florida's Indians. More bibliographic references can be found in my books *Archaeology of Precolumbian Florida* and *Florida Indians and the Invasion from Europe* and in James Covington's *The Seminoles of Florida*, all listed below. Numerous articles on the archaeology and history of Florida's Indians have been published in the *Florida Anthropologist* and the *Florida Historical Quarterly*, journals that are in local libraries and for which subscriptions are available.

Bense, Judith A. *Hawkshaw: Prehistory and History in an Urban Neighborhood in Pensacola, Florida*. Reports of Investigation No. 7. Pensacola: Office of Cultural and Archaeological Research, University of West Florida, 1985.

Clayton, Lawrence A., Vernon James Knight, Jr., and Edward C. Moore, eds. *The De Soto Chronicles: The Expedition of Hernando de Soto to North America in 1539-1543.* 2 vols. Tuscaloosa: University of Alabama Press, 1993.

Covey, Cyclone, ed. and trans. *Alvar Núñez Cabeza de Vaca's Adventures in the Unknown Interior of North America.* Albuquerque: University of New Mexico Press, 1983.

Covington, James W. *The Seminoles of Florida.* Gainesville: University Press of Florida, 1993.

Daniel, I. Randolph, Jr., and Michael Weisenbaker. *Harney Flats: A Florida Paleo-Indian Site.* Farmingdale, N.Y.: Baywood Publishing Co., Inc., 1987.

Davis, Dave D., ed. *Perspectives on Gulf Coast Prehistory.* Gainesville: University of Florida Press, 1984.

Deagan, Kathleen A. *Spanish St. Augustine: The Archaeology of a Colonial Creole Community.* New York: Academic Press, 1983.

Dickinson, Jonathan. *Jonathan Dickinson's Journal; or God's Protecting Providence.* . . . ed. Charles McL. Andrews and Evangeline W. Andrews. Stuart, Fla.: Valentine Books, 1975.

Ewen, Charles R., and John H. Hann. *Hernando de Soto among the Apalachee: The Archaeology of the First Winter Encampment.* Gainesville: University Press of Florida, 1998.

Gannon, Michael V. *The Cross in the Sand: The Early Catholic Church in Florida, 1513-1870.* Reprint. Gainesville: University of Florida Press, 1983.

Gilliland, Marion S. *The Material Culture of Key Marco, Florida.* Gainesville: University of Florida Press, 1975.

Griffin, Patricia C., ed. *Fifty Years of Southeastern Archaeology: Selected Works of John W. Griffin.* Gainesville: University Press of Florida, 1996.

Hann, John H. *Apalachee: The Land between the Rivers.* Gainesville: University of Florida Press, 1988.

———. *Missions to the Calusa.* Gainesville: University of Florida Press, 1991.

———. *History of the Timucua Indians and Missions.* Gainesville: University Press of Florida, 1996.

Hann, John H., and Bonnie G. McEwan. *The Apalachee Indians and Mission San Luis.* Gainesville: University Press of Florida, 1998.

Hudson Charles. *The Southeastern Indians.* Knoxville: University of Tennessee Press, 1976.

Hudson, Charles, and Carmen Chaves Tesser, eds. *The Forgotten Centuries: Indians and Europeans in the American South, 1521-1704.* Athens: University of Georgia Press, 1994.

Lawson, Sarah, and John W. Faupel, eds. *A Foothold in Florida: The Eye-Witness Account of Four Voyages made by the French to that Region.* . . . East Grinstead, Eng.: Antique Atlas Publications, 1992.

Lorant, Stefan. *The New World: The First Pictures of America.* New York: Duell, Sloan, & Pierce, 1946.

Lyon, Eugene. *The Enterprise of Florida: Pedro Menéndez de Avilés and the Spanish Conquest of 1565-1568.* Gainesville: University of Florida Press, 1976.

Marquardt, William H., ed. *Culture and Environment in the Domain of the Calusa.* Institute of Archaeology and Paleoenvironmental Studies, Monograph 1. Gainesville: Florida Museum of Natural History, 1992.

Matter, Robert Allen. *Pre-Seminole Florida: Spanish Soldiers, Friars, and Indian Missions, 1513-1763.* New York: Garland Publishing, 1990.

McEwan, Bonnie G., ed. *Spanish Missions of La Florida.* Gainesville: University Press of Florida, 1993.

McGoun, William E. *Prehistoric People of South Florida.* Tuscaloosa: University of Alabama Press, 1993.

Milanich, Jerald T. *Archaeology of Precolumbian Florida.* Gainesville: University Press of Florida, 1994.

——. *Florida Indians and the Invasion from Europe.* Gainesville: University Press of Florida, 1995.

——. *The Timucua.* Oxford: Blackwell, 1996.

——, ed. *The Hernando de Soto Expedition.* New York: Garland Publishing, 1991.

Milanich, Jerald T., and Charles Hudson. *Hernando de Soto and the Florida Indians.* Gainesville: University Press of Florida, 1993.

Milanich, Jerald T., and Susan Milbrath, eds. *First Encounters: Spanish Explorations in the Caribbean and the United States, 1492-1570.* Gainesville: University of Florida Press, 1989.

Milanich, Jerald T., and Samuel Proctor, eds. *Tacachale: Essays on the Indians of Florida and Southeast Georgia during the Historic Period.* Reprint. Gainesville: University Press of Florida, 1994.

Milanich, Jerald T., and William C. Sturtevant. *Francisco Pareja's 1613 Confessionario: A Documentary Source for Timucuan Ethnography.* Tallahassee: Florida Department of State, 1972.

Milanich, Jerald T., Ann S. Cordell, Vernon J. Knight, Jr., Timothy A. Kohler, and Brenda J. Sigler-Lavelle. *Archaeology of Northern Florida, a.d. 200–900: The McKeithen Weeden Island Culture.* Reprint. Gainesville: University Press of Florida, 1997.

Miller, James J. *An Environmental History of Northeast Florida.* Gainesville: University Press of Florida, 1998.

Purdy, Barbara A. *Florida's Prehistoric Stone Tool Technology: A Study of Flintworking Techniques of Early Florida Stone Implement Makers.* Gainesville: University of Florida Press, 1981.

——. *The Art and Archaeology of Florida's Wetlands.* Boca Raton: CRC Press. 1991.

Scarry, John F., ed. *Political Structure and Change in the Prehistoric Southeastern United States*. Gainesville: University Press of Florida, 1996.

Scarry, Margaret, ed. *Foraging and Farming in the Eastern Woodlands*. Gainesville: University Press of Florida, 1993.

Sears, William H. *Fort Center: An Archaeological Site in the Lake Okeechobee Basin*. Reprint. Gainesville: University Press of Florida, 1994.

Sturtevant, William C., ed. *A Seminole Sourcebook*. New York: Garland Publishing, 1985.

Thomas, David Hurst, ed. *Columbian Consequences*. Vol. 2: *Archaeological and Historical Perspectives on the Spanish Borderlands East*. Washington, D.C.: Smithsonian Institution Press, 1990.

True, David O., ed. *Memoir of D. d'Escalante Fontaneda Respecting Florida, Written in Spain, about the Year 1575*. Coral Gables, Fla.: Glade House, 1945.

Weisman, Brent R. *Like Beads on a String: A Culture History of the Seminole Indians in North Peninsular Florida*. Tuscaloosa: University of Alabama Press, 1989.

————. *Excavations of the Franciscan Frontier: Archaeology of the Fig Springs Mission*. Gainesville: University Press of Florida, 1992.

White, Nancy M., ed. *Archaeology of Northwest Florida and Adjacent Borderlands: Current Research Problems and Approaches*. Florida Anthropological Society Publications No. 11, 1986.

Widmer, Randolph E. *The Evolution of the Calusa: A Nonagricultural Chiefdom on the Southwest Florida Coast*. Tuscaloosa: University of Alabama Press, 1988.

Worth, John E. *The Struggle for the Georgia Coast: An Eighteenth-Century Spanish Retrospect on Guale and Mocama*. Anthropological Papers of the American Museum of Natural History. New York, 1993.

————. *The Timucuan Chiefdoms of Spanish Florida*. Vol. 1: *Assimilation*. Vol. 2: *Resistance and Destruction*. Gainesville: University Press of Florida, 1998.

# Illustration Credits

## Figures

vi Talimali Band, Apalachee Indians of Louisiana, Mr. Gilmer Bennett, chairman; 7 Vertebrate Paleontology Range, Florida Museum of Natural History (FLMNH); 22 FLMNH; 30 W. H. Holmes, "Earthenware of Florida: Collections of Clarence B. Moore," *Journal of the Academy of Natural Sciences of Philadelphia* 10 (1894), figs. 9–12; 45 Clarence B. Moore, "Certain Sand Mounds of the St. John's River, Florida, Part II," *Journal of the Academy of Natural Sciences of Philadelphia* 10 (1894), plate XIX; 48 Theodore de Bry, *Brevis narratio eorum quae in Florida Americae Provincia.* . . . (Frankfurt, 1591), engraving 40; 53 Clarence B. Moore, "Certain Sand Mounds of the St. John's River, Florida, Part I," *Journal of the Academy of Natural Sciences of Philadelphia* 10 (1894), p. 4; 64 Clarence B. Moore, "Certain Sand Mounds of the St. John's River, Part II," p. 165; 85 Gordon R. Willey, *Archeology of the Florida Gulf Coast*, Smithsonian Miscellaneous Collections 113 (Washington, D.C., 1949), p. 461; 88 Florida Division of Historical Resources; and see B. Calvin Jones, "Southern Cult Manifestations at the Lake Jackson Site, Leon County, Florida: Salvage Excavation of Mound 3," *Midcontinental Journal of Archaeology* 7 (1982):31; 99 Clarence B. Moore, "Certain Aboriginal Mounds of the Florida Central West Coast," *Journal of the Academy of Natural Sciences of Philadelphia* 12 (1903), figs. 42, 54, 57–58; 101 Clarence B. Moore, "Certain Aboriginal Mounds of the Florida Central West Coast," fig. 47; 106 FLMNH; 108 George M. Luer, "Mississippian Ceramic Jars, Bottles, and Gourds as Compound Vessels," *Southeastern Archaeology* 15 (1996), fig. 3; 115 (top) FLMNH; 115 (bottom) redrawn from Ross Allen, "The Big Circle Mounds," *Florida Anthropologist* 1 (1948), fig. 7; 121 drawing by Patricia Altman, FLMNH; 125 Department of Anthropology, National Museum of Natural History, Smithsonian Institution, National Museum of Natural History (NMNH); 127 Merald R. Clark, "Faces and Figureheads: The Masks of Prehistoric South Florida" (M.A. thesis, University of Florida, 1995), p. 184; 135 Osvaldo Baldacci, *Atlante Colombiano della Grande Scoperta* (Rome: Instituto Poligraphico e Zecca della Stato, 1992), pp. 123–26; 146 Florida Bureau of Archaeological Research; 149 de Bry, *Brevis narratio*, engraving 10; 151 de Bry, *Brevis narratio*, engraving 13; 162 P. K. Yonge Library of Florida History, University of Florida; 163 Mark F. Boyd, Hale G. Smith, and John W. Griffin, *Here They Once Stood: The Tragic*

*End of the Apalachee Missions* (Gainesville: University of Florida Press, 1951), plate VII; **182** Clay MacCauley, "The Seminole Indians of Florida," *Fifth Annual Report of the Bureau of Ethnology, 1883-84* (Washington, D.C.: Smithsonian Institution, 1889), plate XIX; **183** (top) John M. Goggin Collection, FLMNH; **183** (bottom) Smithsonian Institution, National Anthropological Archives (NAA), Bureau of American Ethnology Collection); **184** (top) John M. Goggin Collection, FLMNH; **184** (bottom) NAA, Deaconess Bedell Collection; **185** FLMNH.

## Plates (following p. 116)

(1) Museum of the American Indians (MIA; presently Smithsonian Institution, National Museum of the American Indian); and see Clarence B. Moore, "Certain Aboriginal Remains of the Northwest Florida Coast, Part II," *Journal of the Academy of Natural Sciences of Philadelphia* 12 (1902), fig. 155; (2) MIA; and see Moore, "Northwest Florida Coast," fig. 54; (3) MIA; and see Moore, "Northwest Florida Coast," fig. 100; (4) Temple Mound Museum, Fort Walton Beach, Florida; and see Yulee W. Lazarus, *The Buck Burial Mound* (Fort Walton Beach, Fla.: Temple Mound Museum, 1979); (5) MIA; and see Moore "Northwest Florida Coast," fig. 23; (6) MIA; and see Moore "Northwest Florida Coast," fig. 4; (7) MIA; and see Moore "Northwest Florida Coast," fig. 215; (8) MIA; and see Clarence B. Moore, "Certain Aboriginal Remains of the Northwest Florida Coast, Part I," *Journal of the Academy of Natural Sciences of Philadelphia* 12 (1901), fig. 70; (9–12) NMNH; (13) FLMNH; (14) FLMNH, Octavia Bryant Stephens and Winston J. T. Stephens Collection; (15) FLMNH; (16) FLMNH.